What a Tee[illegible] W[illegible]s

for easy guitar

Arrangers: Danny Begelman & Pete Sawchuk

Project Manager: Colgan Bryan
Music Editors: Aaron Stang & Colgan Bryan
Technical Editor: Jack Allen
Engraving: MusiComp Inc.
Art Design: Design O' Rama

contents

artist index

...BABY ONE MORE TIME

Words and Music by
MAX MARTIN

Chorus:
Eb
Fm
G7
Cm
Cont. rhy. simile
ba - by, 'cause I need to know now. Oh, be - cause my lone - li - ness is
G7
Eb
Fm
G7
kill - ing me, and I, I must con - fess I still be - lieve (still be - lieve
To Coda
Cm
G7
Ab
Bb
Eb
1.
Fm
G7
) that when I'm not with you I lose my mind. Give me a sign. Hit me, ba - by, one more time.
2.
Fm
N.C.
Piano (arr. for gtr.)
Hit me, ba - by, one more time. Oh, ba - by, ba - by. Oh, ba - by, ba - by.
Bridge:
Cm
G7
Eb
Elec. Gtr.
Oh, ba - by, ba - by, how was I sup - posed to know?
Fm
G7sus
G7
Abmaj7
Bb
Fm
Oh, pret - ty ba - by, I should - n't have let you go.

Ab
Bb
Cm
G7
Resume verse fig. simile
I must con - fess that my lone - li - ness is kill - ing me now.
Eb
Fm
G7sus
G7
Ab
Don't you know I still be - lieve that you will be here
Bb
Abmaj7
Eb/G
Fm
Bb
G/B
D.S. al Coda
and give me a sign.
Hit me, ba - by, one more time.
Coda
Fm
G7
Cm
G7
Hit me, ba - by, one more time.
I must con - fess that my lone - li - ness is kill - ing me now.
Eb
Fm
G7
Cm
Don't you know I still be - lieve that you will be here
G7
Ab
Bb
Eb
Fm
G7sus
Cm
Elec. Gtr.
and give me a sign.
Hit me, ba - by, one more time.

BE WITH YOU

Words and Music by
ENRIQUE IGLESIAS,
PAUL BARRY and MARK TAYLOR

Verse 1:
E
B
C#m
Mon-day night, and I feel so low. I count the hours, but they
G#m
A
go so slow. I know the
C#m
sound of your voice is in my soul.
Verses 2 & 3:
E
B
C#m
Cont. rhy. simile
2. Cit - y lights and streets of gold. Look out my win-dow to the
3. I can't sleep; I'm up all night. Through these tears, I
*Acous. Gtr. 1
*Verse 3 only.
G#m
A
world be - low. Moves so fast, but it feels so cold and I'm
try to smile. I know the touch of your hand can

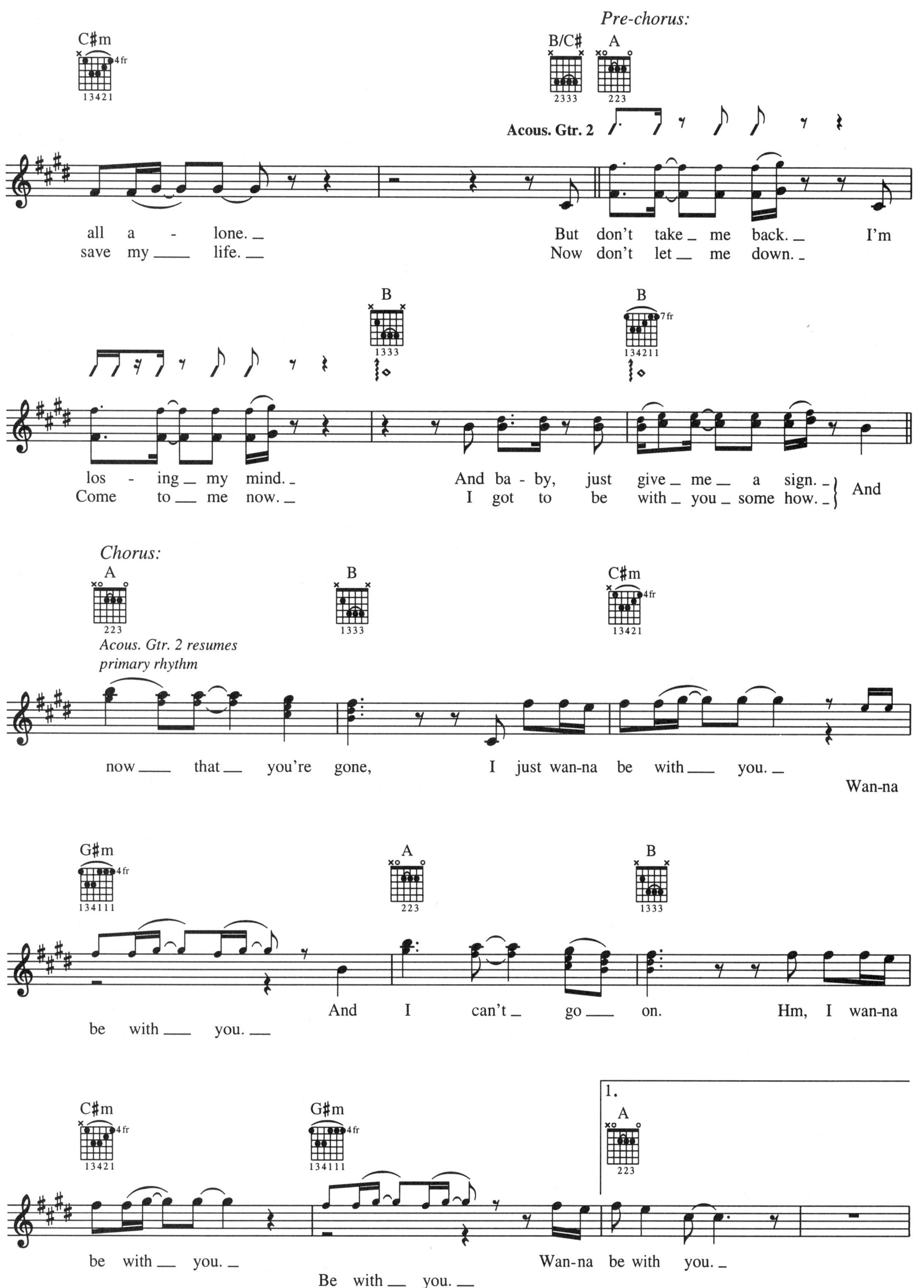
Pre-chorus:
C♯m
B/C♯
A
Acous. Gtr. 2
all a - lone.
save my life.
But don't take me back. I'm
Now don't let me down.
B
los - ing my mind.
Come to me now.
And ba - by, just give me a sign.
I got to be with you some how.
And
Chorus:
A
B
C♯m
Acous. Gtr. 2 resumes primary rhythm
now that you're gone, I just wan-na be with you.
Wan-na
G♯m
A
B
And I can't go on. Hm, I wan-na
be with you.
C♯m
G♯m
1.
A
be with you. Wan-na be with you.
Be with you.

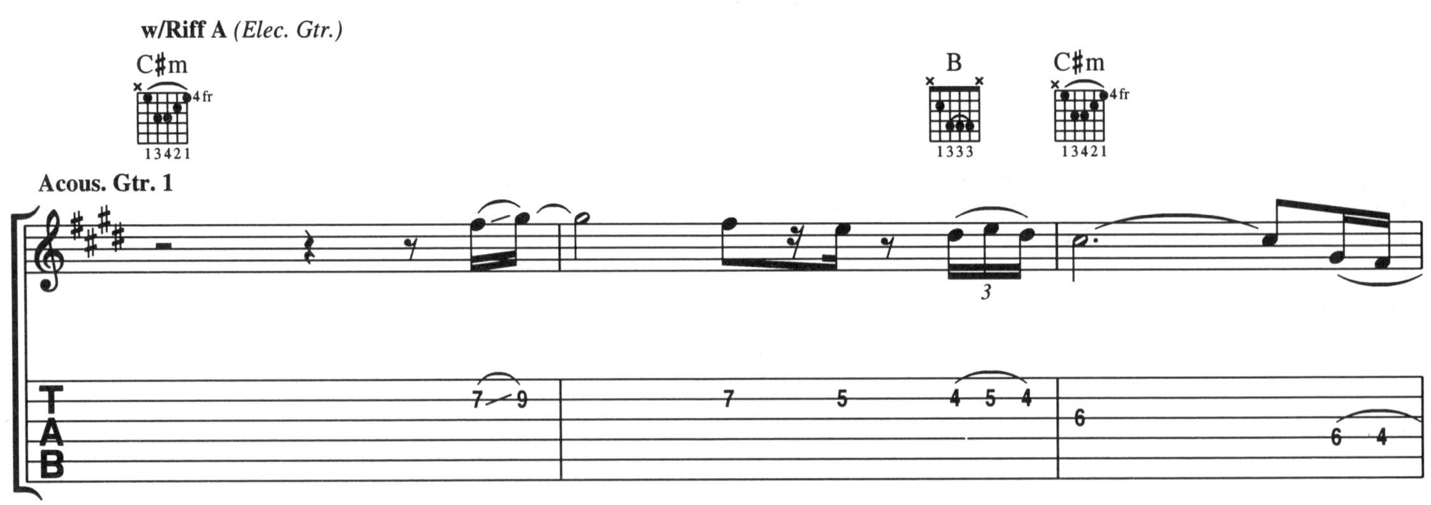
w/Riff A (Elec. Gtr.)
C♯m
B
C♯m
Acous. Gtr. 1

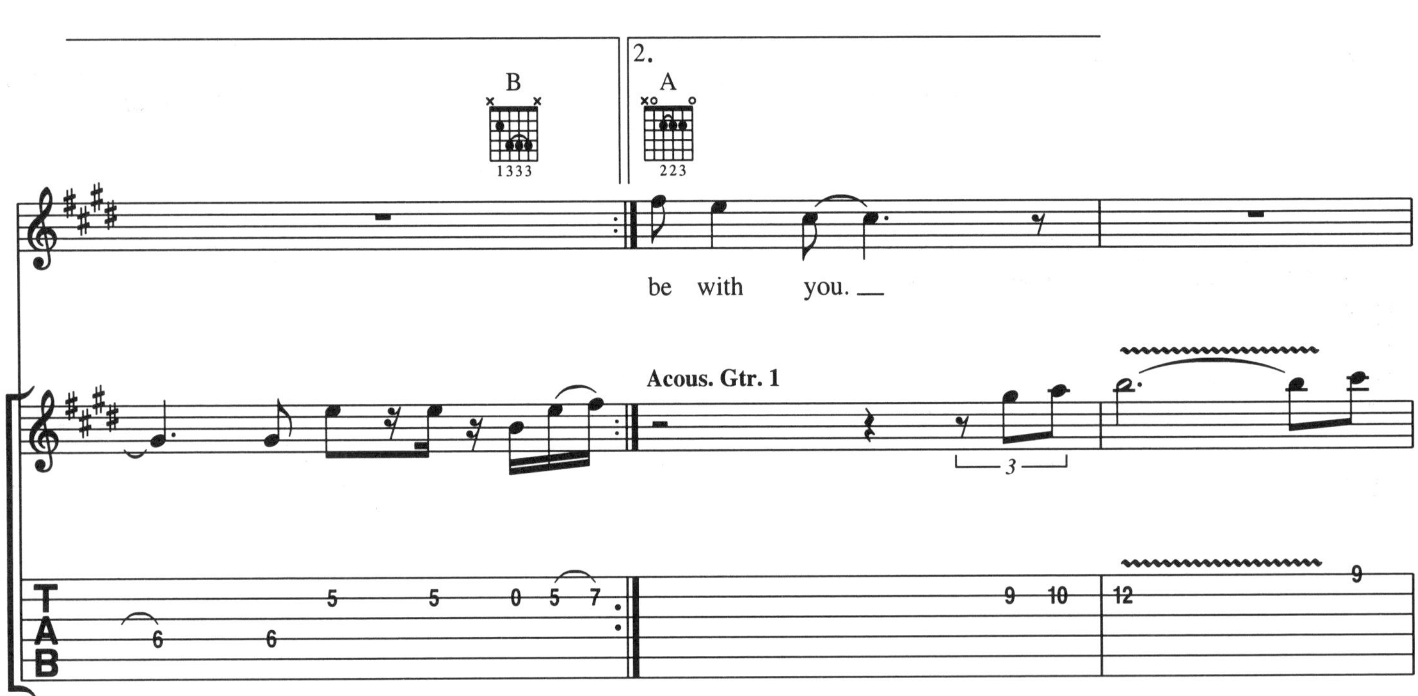
B
2.
A
be with you.
Acous. Gtr. 1

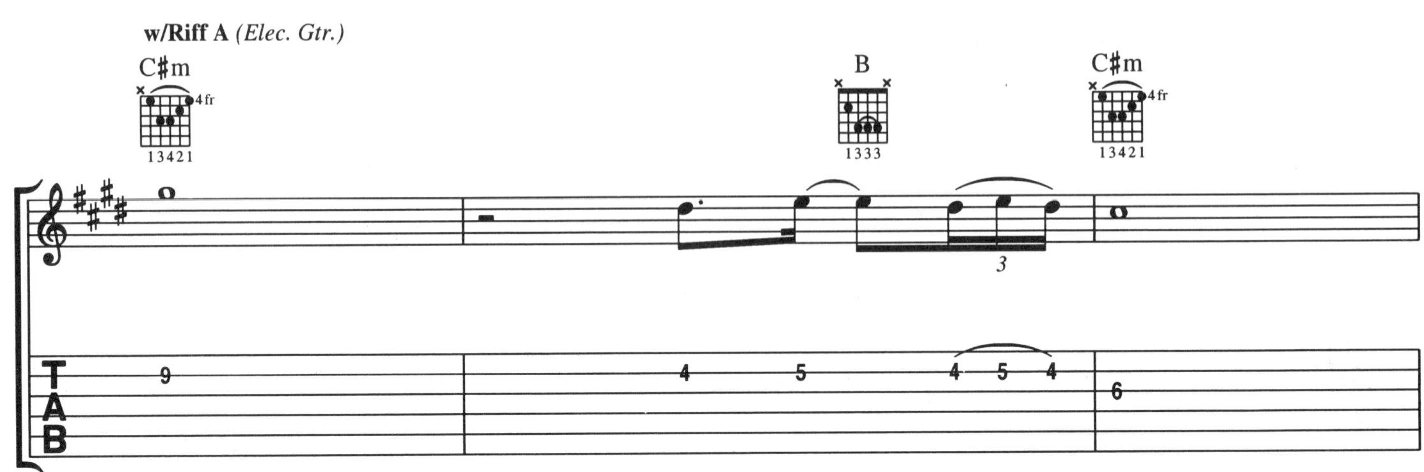
w/Riff A (Elec. Gtr.)
C♯m
B
C♯m

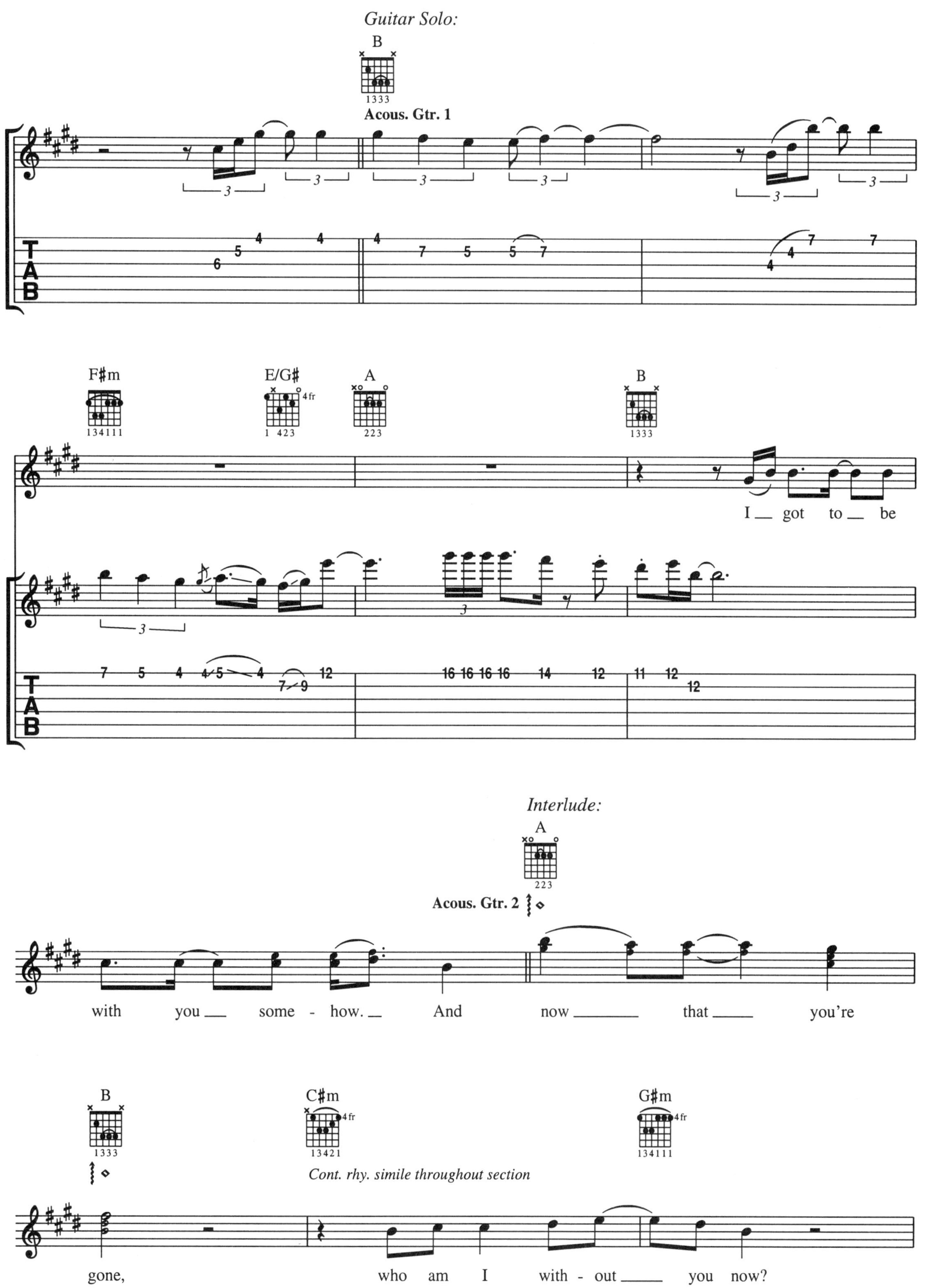
Guitar Solo:
B
1333
Acous. Gtr. 1
F♯m
134111
E/G♯
4 fr
1 423
A
223
B
1333
I got to be
Interlude:
A
223
Acous. Gtr. 2
with you some - how. And now that you're
B
1333
C♯m
4fr
13421
G♯m
4fr
134111
Cont. rhy. simile throughout section
gone, who am I with - out you now?

A
B
C♯m
223
1333
13421
4 fr
I can't go on; I just wan-na be with you.
Acous. Gtr. 1
T
A
B
7 5
Chorus:
G♯m
A
B
134111
223
1333
4 fr
Acous. Gtr. 2 resumes primary rhythm
And now that you're gone, I just wan-na
Be with you.
*Acous. Gtr. 1
7 7 9 9
5 4
*Ad lib. simile 2nd time.
C♯m
G♯m
A
13421
134111
223
4 fr
be with you.
And I can't go
Wan-na be with you.
5 0
6 4 5 7 5 4 5 4
6 4 5

1.
B
C♯m
G♯m
on. Hm, I wan-na be with you, wan - na be with
Be with you.
2.
Outro:
A
be with you, woah.
Just wan-na be with you.
**Acous. Gtr. 1
**Ad lib. simile on repeats.
Just wan-na be with you.
Repeat and fade

BECAUSE OF YOU

Words and Music by
ANDERS BAGGE, ARNTHOR BIRGISSON,
CHRISTIAN KARLSSON and PATRICK TUCKER

Verse:
C
G/B
Dm7
Cont. rhy. simile
- shine.
Oh. __
1. Ba - by, I real - ly know by now. Since we met
2. Hon - est - ly, to be with me like it was
Am
G
F
C/E
that day you showed me the way. I felt it then, you gave me love I can't de - scribe how much __
be - fore need to lis - ten more. 'Cause when I close my eyes at night, I re - al - ize that no one else could ev -
__ I feel __ for you. __ I said, "Ba - by, I should have known
- er take __ your place. __ I still can feel, and it's so __
by now," __ should have been right there when - ev - er you gave me love. __ And if
__ real __ when you're touch - ing me, kiss - es end - less - ly. __ It's just the
1.
on - ly you were __ here, __ I'd tell __ you, yes, I'd tell __ you, oh yeah. _ You're my
place in the sun where our love's _ be - gun. I miss _ you, yes, I miss _
2.
Chorus:
__ you, oh babe. _ You're my sun - shine af - ter the rain. _ You're the cure a - gainst my fear and my pain. _

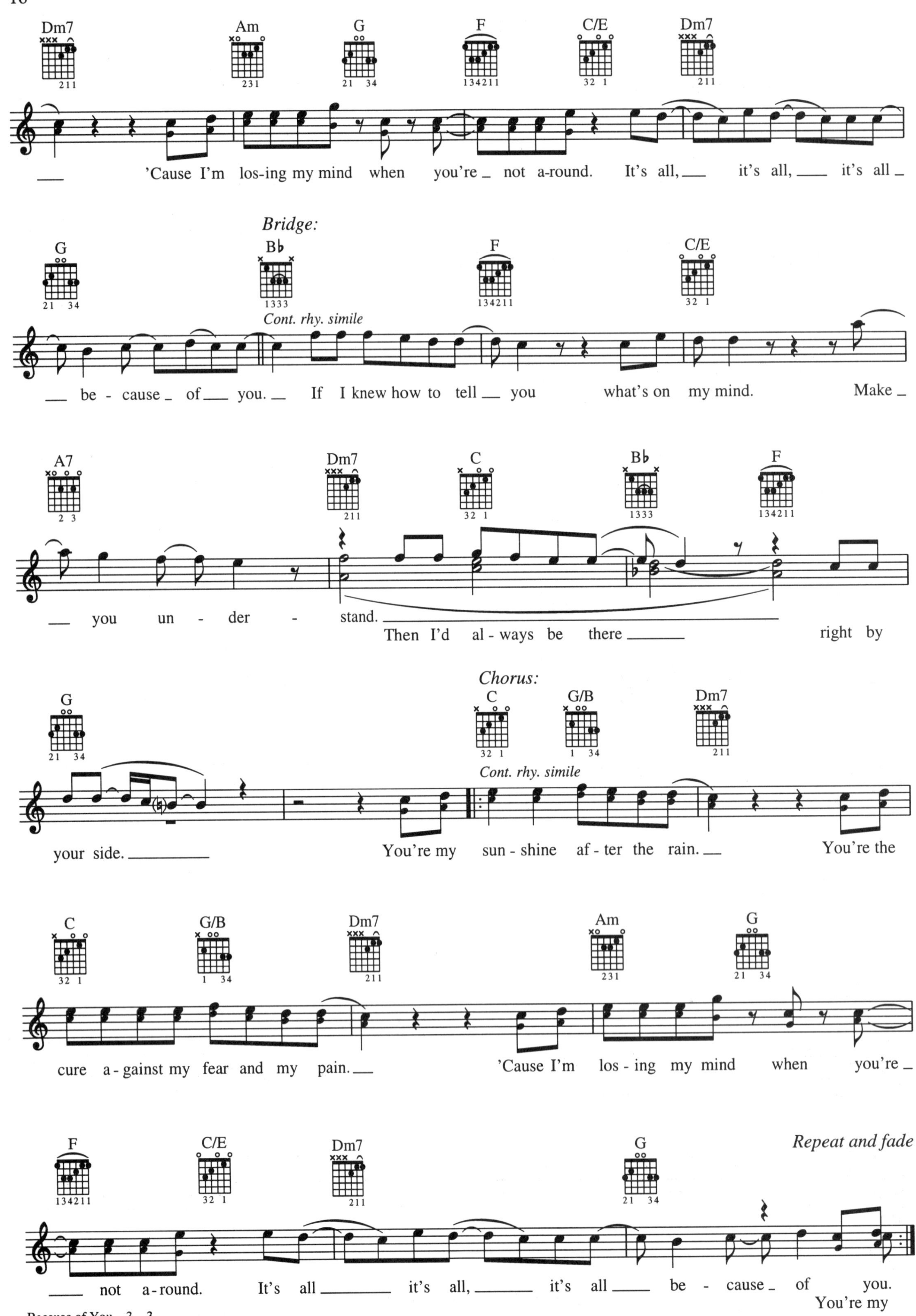
Dm7
Am
G
F
C/E
Dm7
'Cause I'm los-ing my mind when you're not a-round. It's all, it's all, it's all
Bridge:
G
B♭
F
C/E
Cont. rhy. simile
be - cause of you. If I knew how to tell you what's on my mind. Make
A7
Dm7
C
B♭
F
you un - der - stand.
Then I'd al - ways be there right by
Chorus:
G
C
G/B
Dm7
Cont. rhy. simile
your side. You're my sun - shine af - ter the rain. You're the
C
G/B
Dm7
Am
G
cure a - gainst my fear and my pain. 'Cause I'm los - ing my mind when you're
F
C/E
Dm7
G
Repeat and fade
not a - round. It's all it's all, it's all be - cause of you.
You're my

BLESSED

Words and Music by
TRAVON POTTS and BROCK WALSH

Verse:
w/Rhy. Fig. 1 (Acous. Gtr.)
G/B
C
Em7
F
1. When I think how life used to be. Al - ways walk - ing in the shad - ows. Then I look at what you've giv - en me, I feel like danc - ing on my tip - toes.
2. There are times that test your faith 'til you think you might sur - ren - der. Ba - by, I'm, I'm not a - shamed to say that my hopes were grow - ing slen - der.
Pre-chorus:
Dm7
Em7
Am7
F/B♭
F/G
Acous. Gtr.
I must say ev-'ry day I wake and re - a - lize you're by my side. I know I'm tru - ly
You walked by in the nick of time, look - ing like an an - swered prayer. You know I'm tru - ly
Deep in - side of me you fill me with your gen - tle touch. You know I'm tru - ly
Chorus:
w/Rhy. Fig. 1 (Acous. Gtr.)
blessed for ev - 'ry - thing you give me, blessed for all the

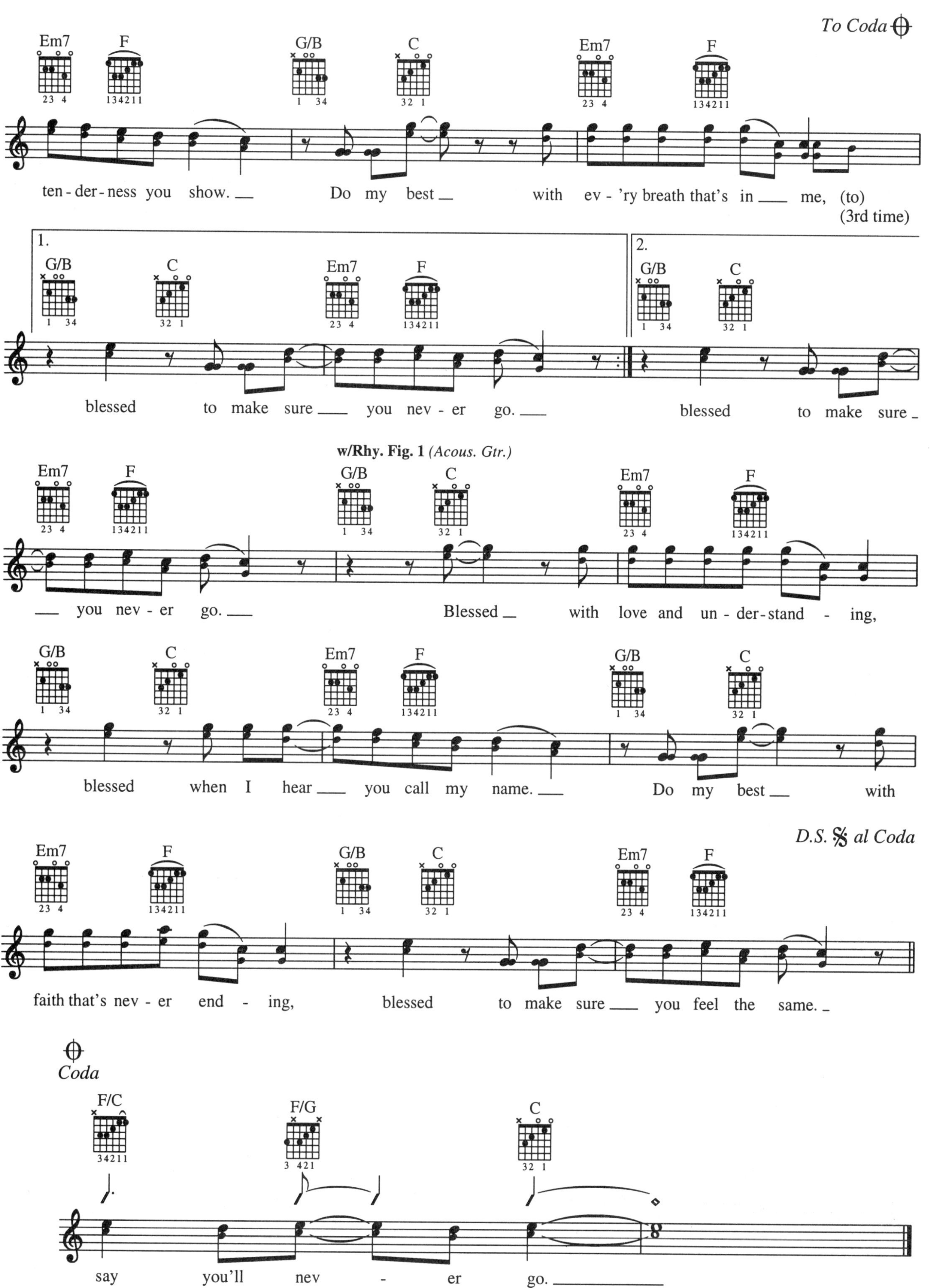
To Coda
Em7
F
G/B
C
tenderness you show. Do my best with ev-'ry breath that's in me, (to)
(3rd time)
1.
2.
blessed to make sure you never go.
blessed to make sure
w/Rhy. Fig. 1 (Acous. Gtr.)
you never go. Blessed with love and understanding,
blessed when I hear you call my name. Do my best with
D.S. al Coda
faith that's never ending, blessed to make sure you feel the same.
Coda
F/C
F/G
say you'll never go.

BLUE (DA BA DEE)

Music by LOBIAN, RANDONE
Words by GABUTTI, LOBINA

Tune down 1/2 step:
⑥= E♭ ③= G♭
⑤= A♭ ②= B♭
④= D♭ ①= E♭

Moderate dance beat ♩ = 120

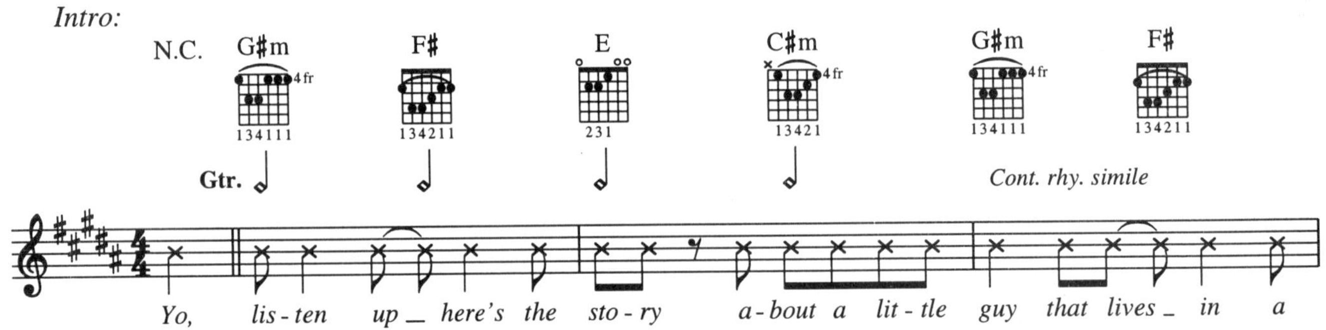
Intro:
N.C. G♯m F♯ E C♯m G♯m F♯
Gtr.
Cont. rhy. simile
Yo, lis - ten up _ here's the sto - ry a - bout a lit - tle guy that lives _ in a

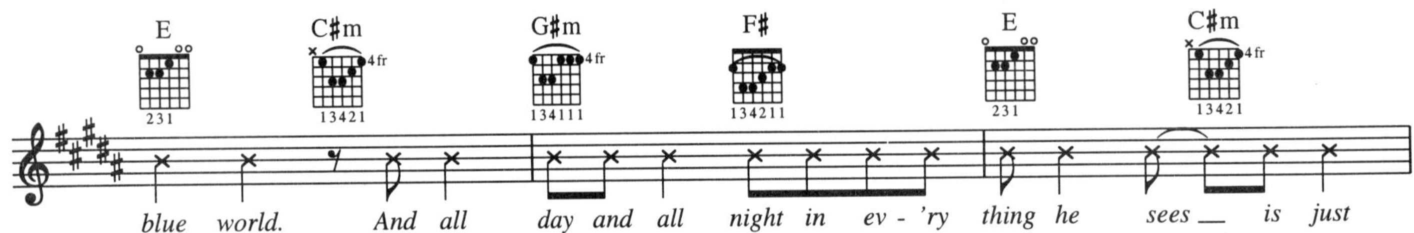
E C♯m G♯m F♯ E C♯m
blue world. And all day and all night in ev - 'ry thing he sees _ is just

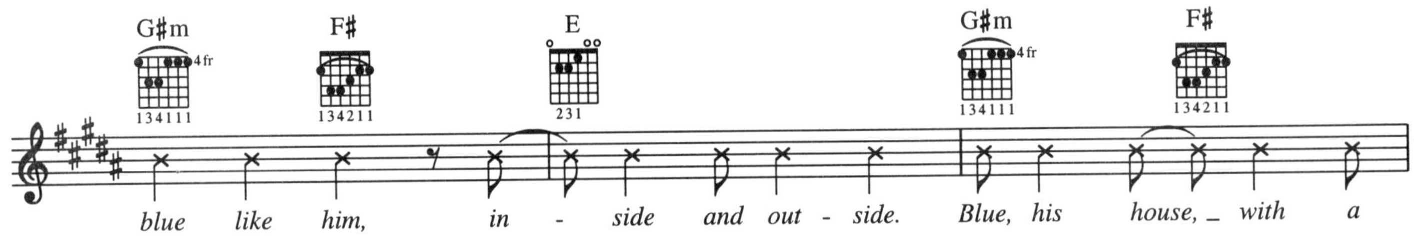
G♯m F♯ E G♯m F♯
blue like him, in - side and out - side. Blue, his house, _ with a

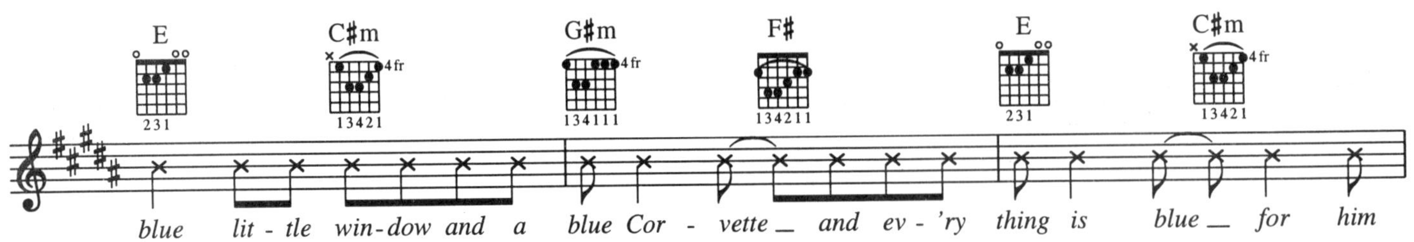
E C♯m G♯m F♯ E C♯m
blue lit - tle win - dow and a blue Cor - vette _ and ev - 'ry thing is blue _ for him

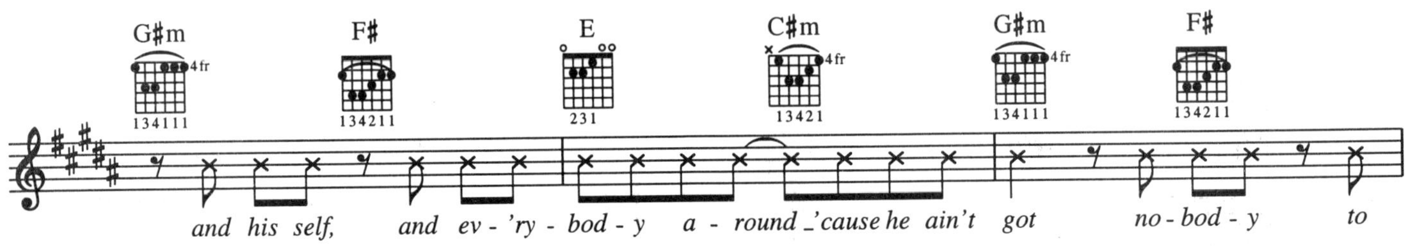
G♯m F♯ E C♯m G♯m F♯
and his self, and ev - 'ry - bod - y a - round _ 'cause he ain't got no - bod - y to

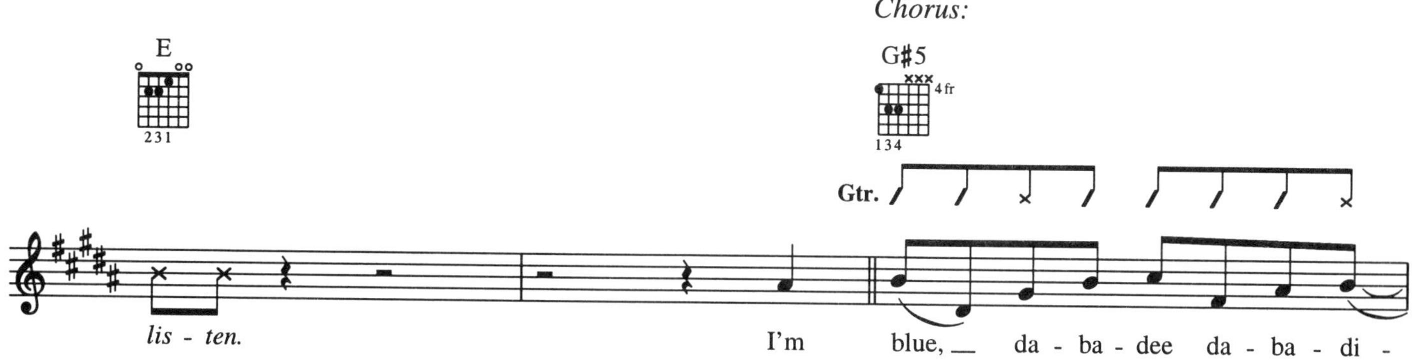
Chorus:
E
231
G#5
4 fr
134
Gtr.
lis - ten.
I'm
blue, da - ba - dee da - ba - di -

Cont. rhy. simile
- da - ba - dee - da - ba - di - da - ba - dee - da - ba - di - da - ba - dee - da - ba -

di - da - ba - dee - da - ba - di - da - ba - dee da - ba - di - da - ba - dee da - ba - di.

G#m
134111
4fr
F#
134211
E
231
C#m
13421
4fr
I'm
blue, da - ba - dee - da - ba - di - da - ba - dee - da - ba -

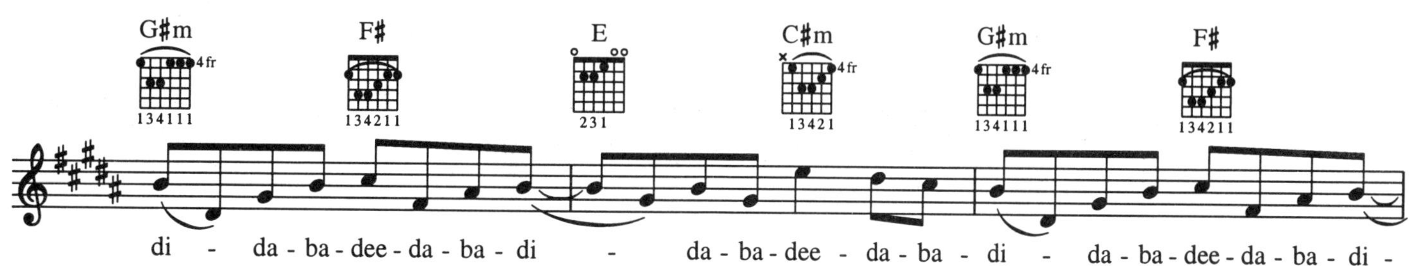
G#m
F#
E
C#m
G#m
F#
di - da - ba - dee - da - ba - di - da - ba - dee - da - ba - di - da - ba - dee - da - ba - di -

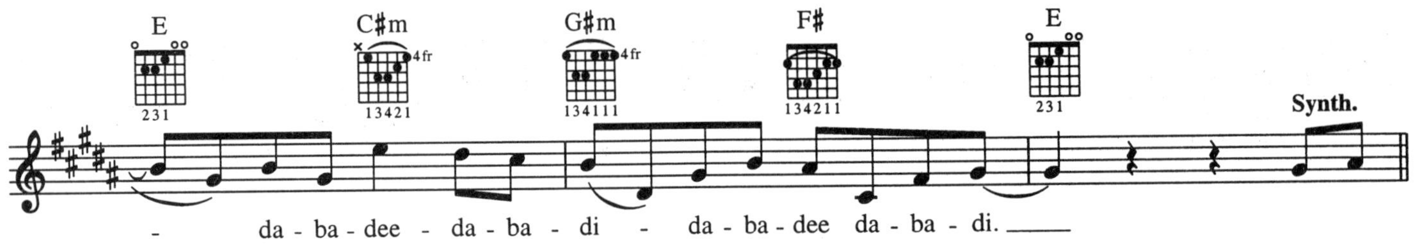
E
C♯m
4fr
G♯m
4fr
F♯
E
231
13421
134111
134211
231
Synth.
- da - ba - dee - da - ba - di - da - ba - dee da - ba - di.

Interlude:

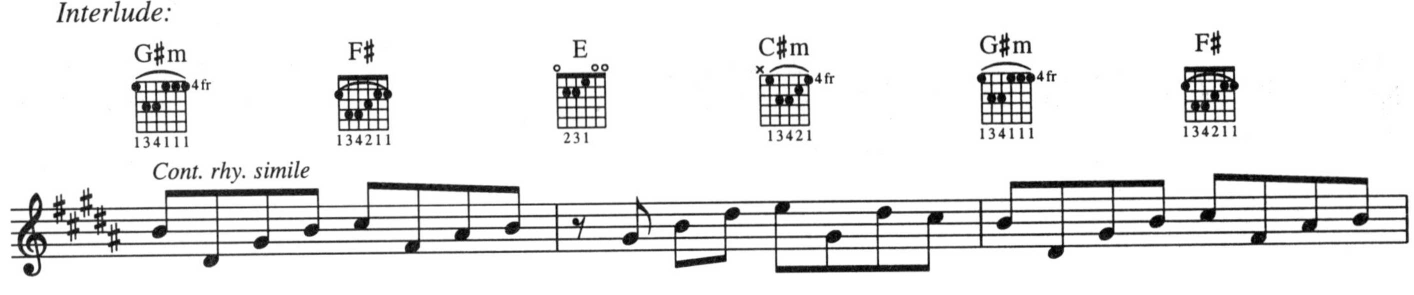
G♯m
F♯
E
C♯m
G♯m
F♯
4fr
134111
134211
231
13421
134111
134211
Cont. rhy. simile

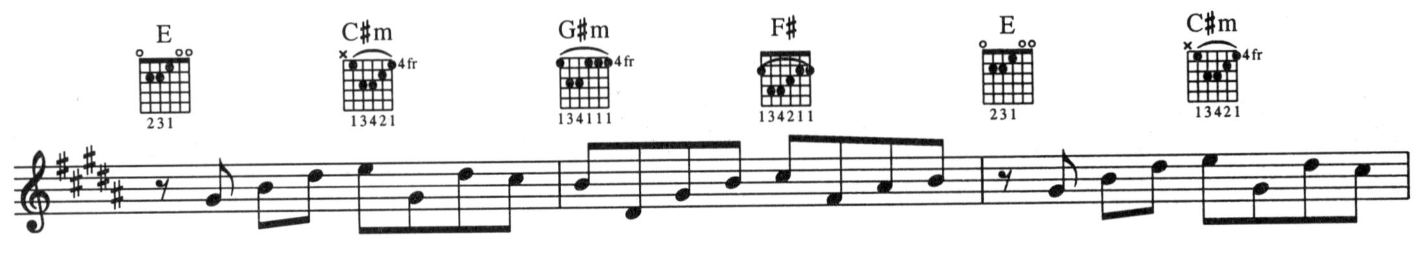
E
C♯m
G♯m
F♯
E
C♯m
4fr
231
13421
134111
134211
231
13421

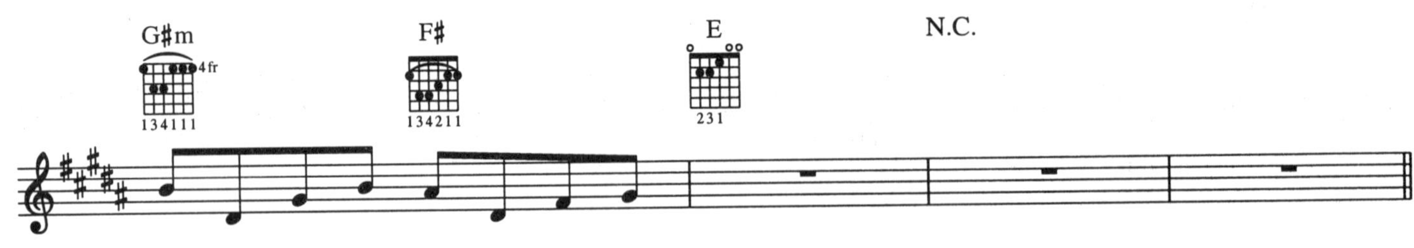
G♯m
F♯
E
N.C.
4fr
134111
134211
231

Verse:

(D♯m)
I have a blue house with a blue win-dow.
Blue is the col - or of

all that I wear.
Blue are the streets and all the trees are too.

D♯m
6fr
13421
Gtr.
I have a girl-friend and she is so blue.
Blue are the peo-ple here that

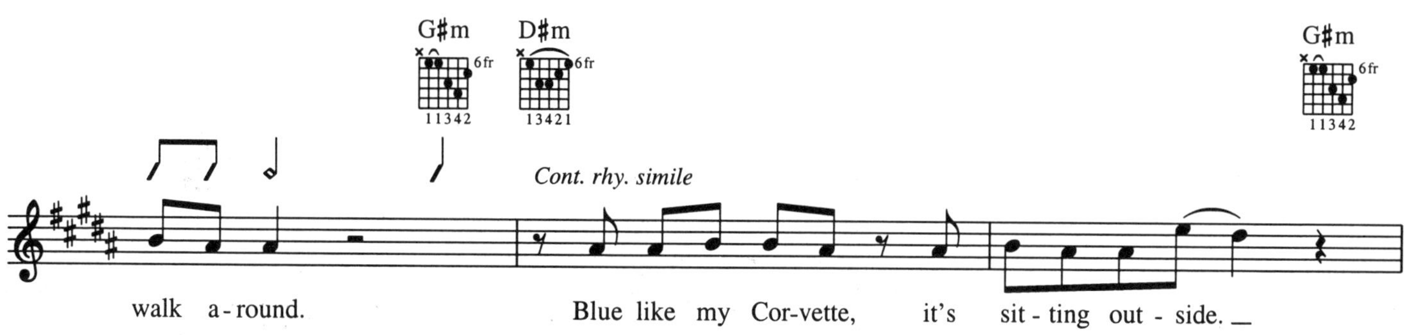
G♯m
6fr
11342
D♯m
6fr
13421
Cont. rhy. simile
G♯m
6fr
11342
walk a-round.
Blue like my Cor-vette, it's sit-ting out-side.

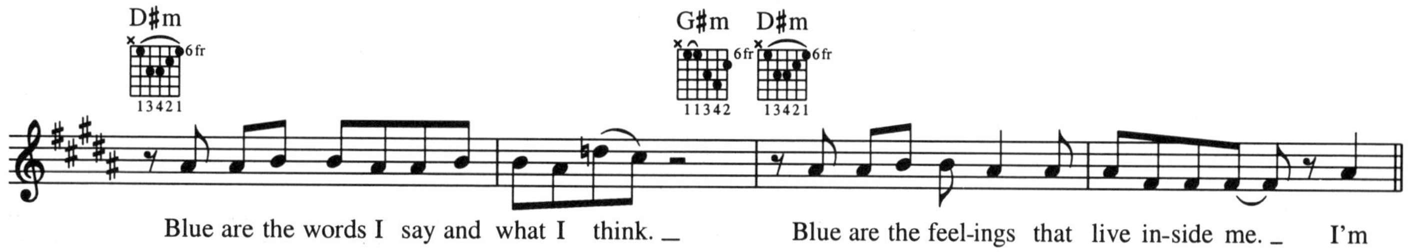
D♯m
6fr
13421
G♯m
6fr
11342
D♯m
6fr
13421
Blue are the words I say and what I think.
Blue are the feel-ings that live in-side me. I'm

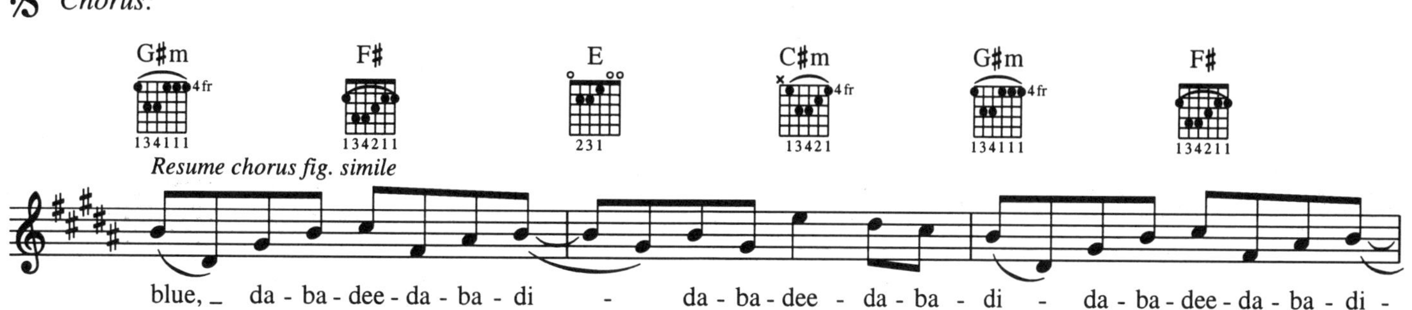
Chorus:
G♯m
4fr
134111
F♯
134211
E
231
C♯m
4fr
13421
G♯m
4fr
134111
F♯
134211
Resume chorus fig. simile
blue, da-ba-dee-da-ba-di - da-ba-dee - da-ba - di - da-ba-dee-da-ba-di -

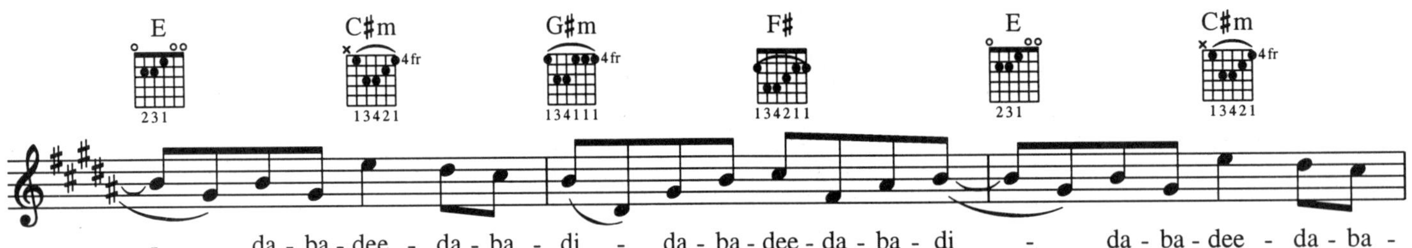
E
C♯m
G♯m
F♯
E
C♯m
- da - ba - dee - da - ba - di - da - ba - dee - da - ba - di - da - ba - dee - da - ba -

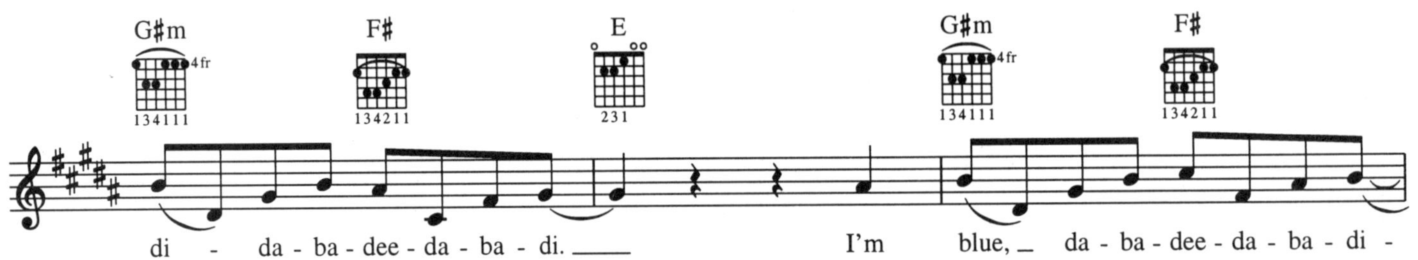
G♯m
F♯
E
G♯m
F♯
di - da - ba - dee - da - ba - di. I'm blue, da - ba - dee - da - ba - di -

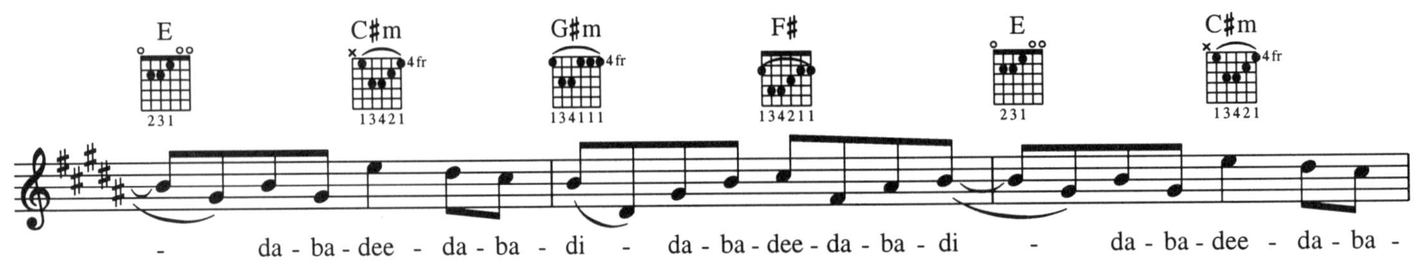
E
C♯m
G♯m
F♯
E
C♯m
- da - ba - dee - da - ba - di - da - ba - dee - da - ba - di - da - ba - dee - da - ba -

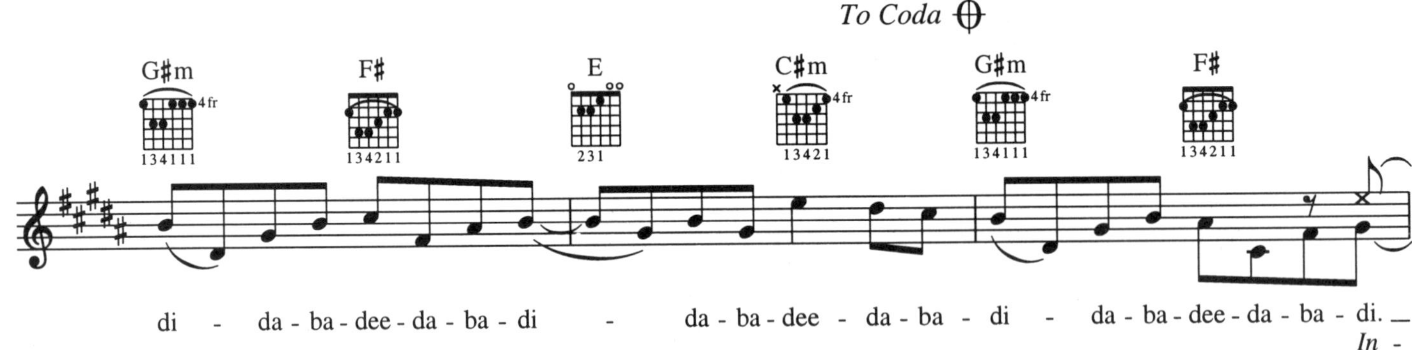
To Coda
G♯m
F♯
E
C♯m
G♯m
F♯
di - da - ba - dee - da - ba - di - da - ba - dee - da - ba - di - da - ba - dee - da - ba - di.
In -

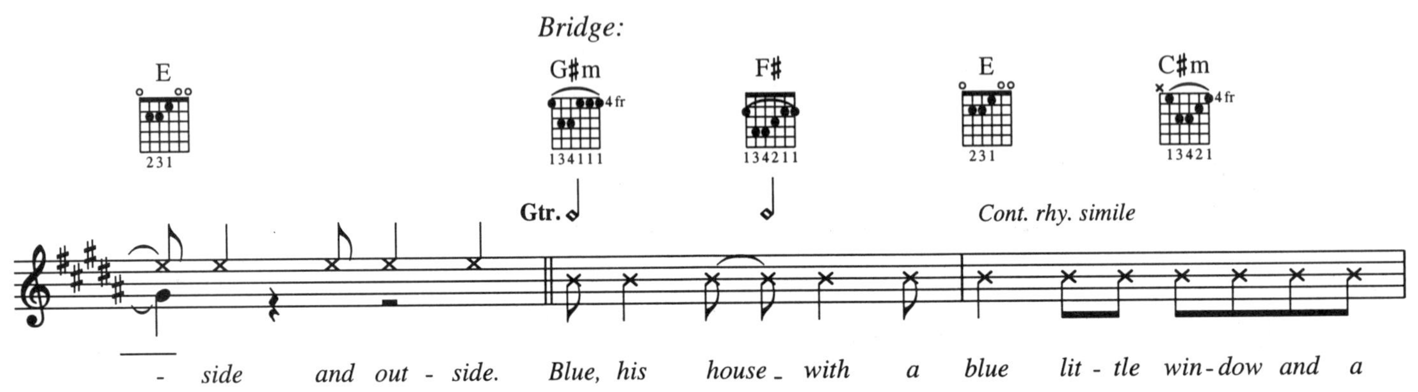
Bridge:
E
G♯m
F♯
E
C♯m
Gtr.
Cont. rhy. simile
- side and out - side. Blue, his house with a blue lit - tle win - dow and a

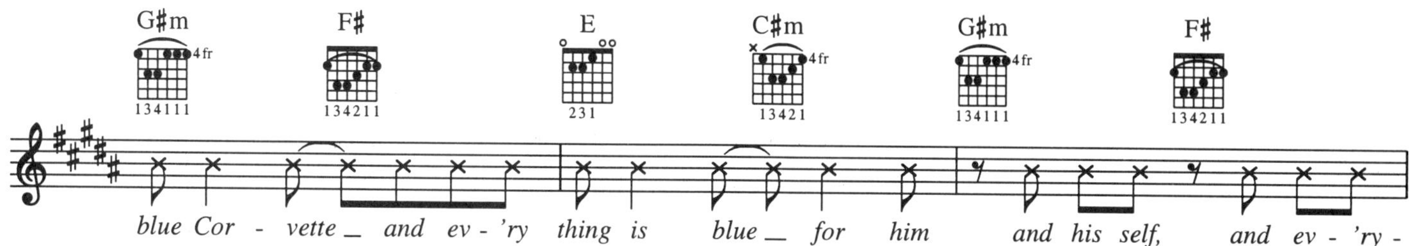
G♯m
F♯
E
C♯m
G♯m
F♯
blue Cor - vette _ and ev - 'ry thing is blue _ for him and his self, and ev - 'ry -

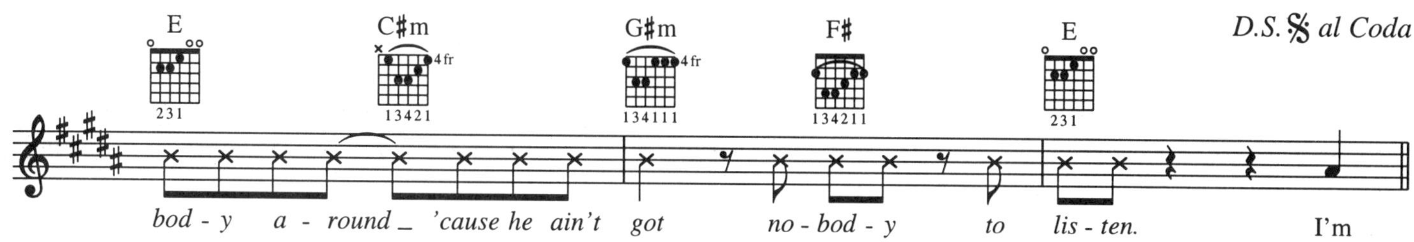
E
C♯m
G♯m
F♯
E
D.S. 𝄋 al Coda
bod - y a - round _ 'cause he ain't got no - bod - y to lis - ten. I'm

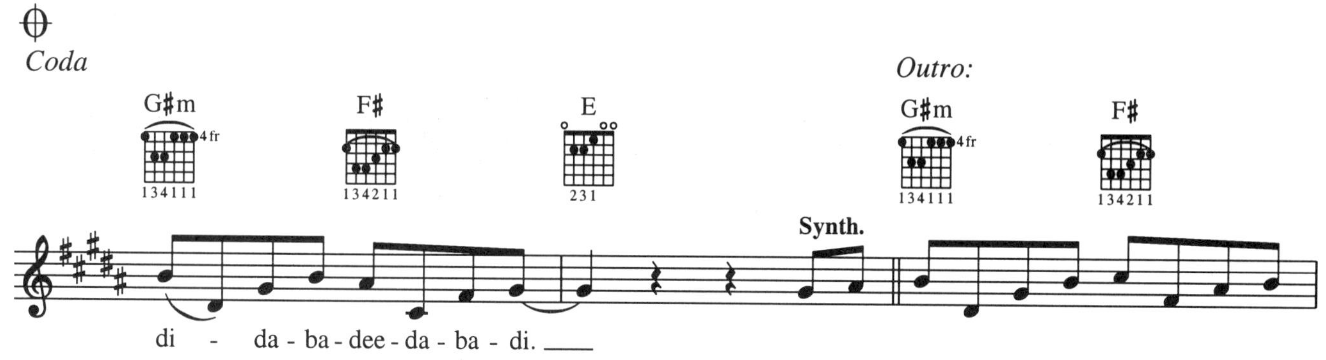
Coda
Outro:
G♯m
F♯
E
G♯m
F♯
Synth.
di - da - ba - dee - da - ba - di. ___

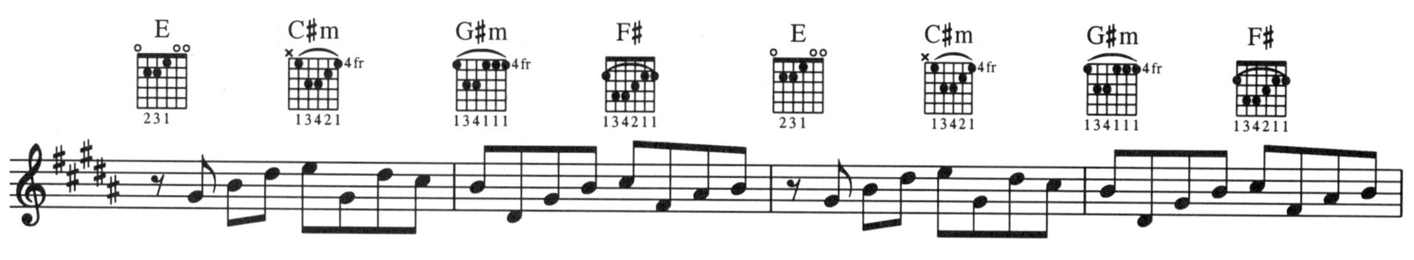
E
C♯m
G♯m
F♯
E
C♯m
G♯m
F♯

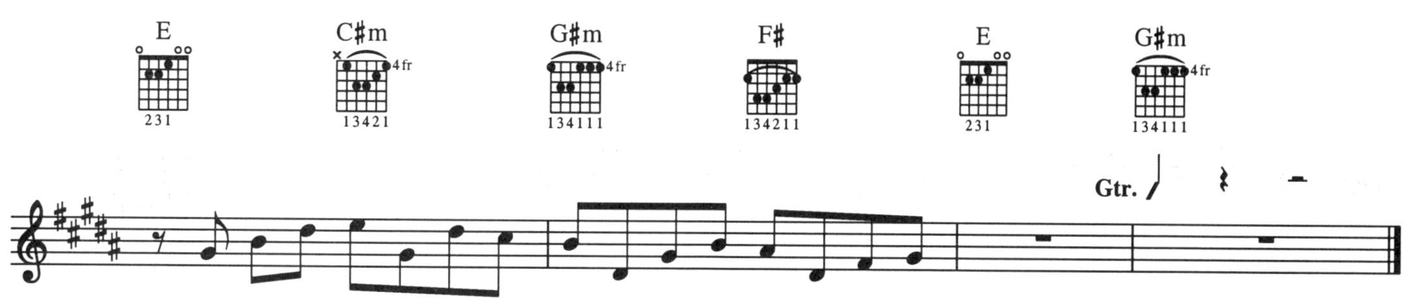
E
C♯m
G♯m
F♯
E
G♯m
Gtr.

BYE BYE BYE

Words and Music by KRISTIAN LUNDIN,
JAKE and ANDREAS CARLSSON

Pre-chorus:
E
231
F♯
134211
Cont. rhy. simile
I know that I can't take no more, it ain't no lie.
E
231
D♯7
1324
I wan - na see you out that door, ba - by, bye - bye - bye. Bye -
Chorus:
G♯m
4fr
134111
F♯
134211
Cont. rhy. simile
bye. Don't wan-na be a fool for you, just an-oth-er play-er in your game or two.
E
231
D♯7
1324
You may hate me but it ain't no lie, ba - by, bye - bye - bye. Bye -
G♯m
4fr
134111
F♯
134211
bye. Don't real-ly wan-na make it tough, I just wan-na tell you that I had e-nough.
To Coda
E
231
D♯7
1324
E
231
F♯
134211
Might sound cra - zy but it ain't no lie. Ba - by, bye - bye - bye.
(3rd time) Bye -

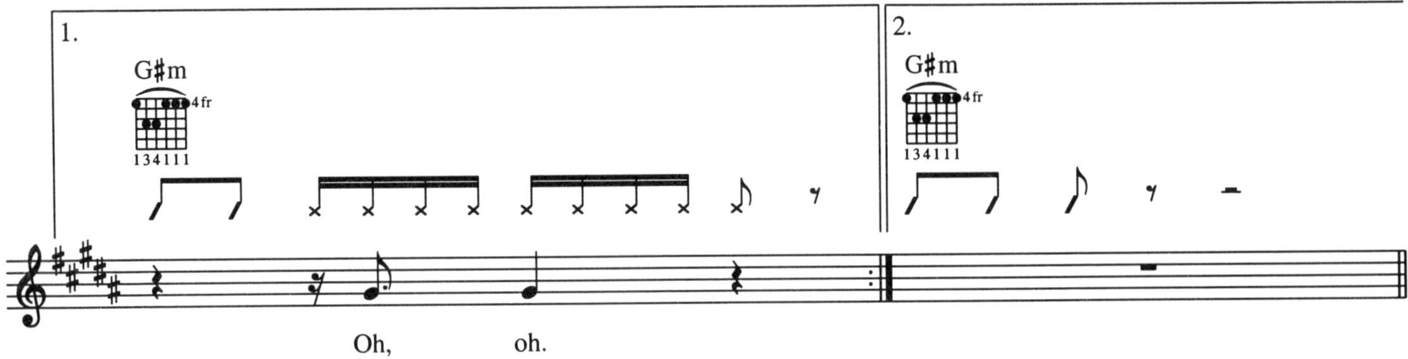
1.
G♯m
4fr
134111
2.
G♯m
4fr
134111
Oh, oh.

Bridge:

I'm giv-ing up, I know for sure. I don't wan-na be the rea-son for your love no more. Bye -

bye. I'm check-ing out, I'm sign - ing off, I don't wan-na be the los - er and I've had e-nough.

Interlude:

F♯ 134211 — E 231

w/Synth.

I don't wan - na be ___ your fool ___ in this game for two ___ so I'm

D♯7 1324 — G♯m 4fr 134111 — F♯ 134211

Elec. Gtr. *Cont. rhy. simile*

leav - ing you be - hind. ___ I don't wan - na make _ it tough _ but I've

E 231 — D♯7 1324 — *D.S. 𝄋 al Coda* — 𝄌 *Coda* G♯m 4fr 134111

Elec. Gtr.

had e - nough _ and it ain't no lie, bye-bye. bye.

DON'T WANNA LOSE YOU NOW

Words and Music by
MAX MARTIN

Tune down 1/2 step:
⑥= E♭ ③= G♭
⑤= A♭ ②= B♭
④= D♭ ①= E♭

Moderately ♩ = 92
Intro:
N.C.
Em
Am
F
C/G
Gsus
G
Acous. Gtr.
mf
Cont. in slashes
Verses 1 & 2:
Acous. Gtr.
Cont. rhy. simile
1. I nev - er thought that I would lose my mind, that I could con - trol this. Nev - er thought that I'd be left be - hind, that I was strong - er than you. (Ba - by.) Girl if on - ly I knew
2. I've got this feel - ing you're not gon - na stay, it's burn - ing with - in me. The fear of los - ing, of slip - ping a - way, it just keeps get - ting clos - er. (Ba - by.) What - ev - er rea - son to leave

Am
F
G
what I've done, you know, so why don't you tell me. (And I
that I had, my place is al - ways be - side you. And I
Em
Am
F
G
) I would bring down the moon and the sun to show how much I care.
wish that I did - n't need you so bad, your face just won't go a - way.
Don't wan-na lose
Chorus:
Em
Am
F
C/G
G
Cont. rhy. simile
you now, ba - by, I know we can win this. Don't wan - na lose
Em
Am
F
C/G
1.
Gsus
G
you now, no, no, or ev - er a - gain.
(Lose you now.)
2.
Gsus
G
Em
Am
F
C
Don't wan - na lose you now. (Don't wan - na lose you now.)
Verse 3:
G
Am
F
Acous. Gtr.
Cont. rhy. simile
I nev - er thought that I would lose my mind, that I could con - trol

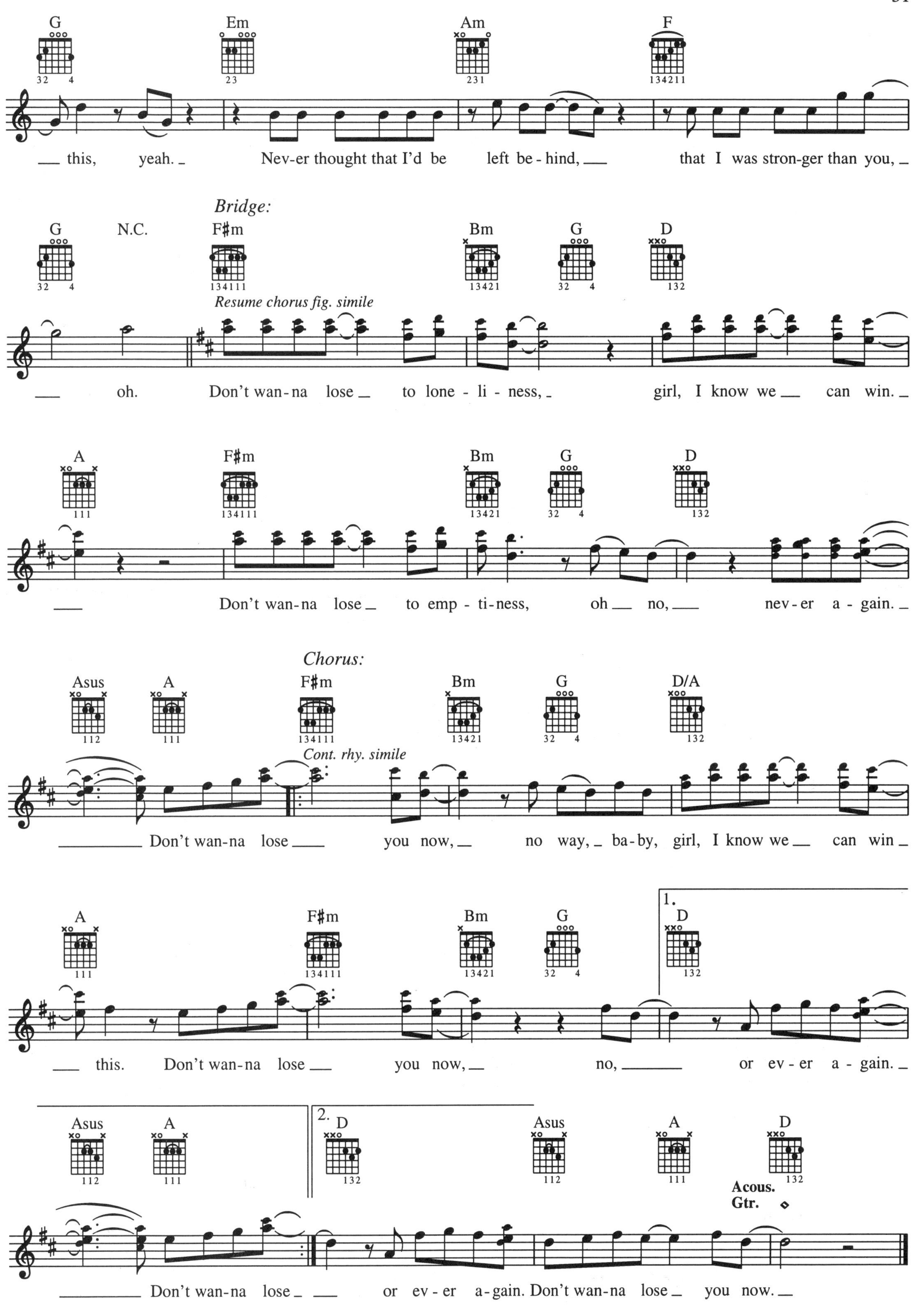
G
Em
Am
F
this, yeah. Nev-er thought that I'd be left be-hind, that I was stron-ger than you,
Bridge:
G
N.C.
F♯m
Bm
G
D
Resume chorus fig. simile
oh. Don't wan-na lose to lone-li-ness, girl, I know we can win.
A
F♯m
Bm
G
D
Don't wan-na lose to emp-ti-ness, oh no, nev-er a-gain.
Chorus:
Asus
A
F♯m
Bm
G
D/A
Cont. rhy. simile
Don't wan-na lose you now, no way, ba-by, girl, I know we can win
A
F♯m
Bm
G
1.
D
this. Don't wan-na lose you now, no, or ev-er a-gain.
Asus
A
2.
D
Asus
A
D
Acous. Gtr.
Don't wan-na lose or ev-er a-gain. Don't wan-na lose you now.

FROM THE BOTTOM OF MY BROKEN HEART

Words and Music by
ERIC FOSTER WHITE

Verse:
Em7
D/F♯
G
Am7
C
D
*Nylon-Str. Gtrs. 1 & 2
Cont. rhy. simile
1. "Nev - er look back," we said. How was I to know I'd miss you so?
2. "Ba - by," I said, "please stay. Give our love a chance for one more day."
*Two gtrs. arr. for one.
G
C/D
Em7
D/F♯
G
Am7
Lone - li - ness up a - head. emp - ti - ness be -
We could have worked things out. Tak - ing time is
C
D
G
Em
hind, where do I go? And you did - n't have all my joy
what love's all a - bout. But you put a dart through my dreams,
Em(maj7)
Em7
through my tears, all my hopes through my fears, did you now?
through my heart, and I'm back where I start - ed a - gain.
A9
Am7
C/D
Nylon-str. Gtrs. 1 & 2
Still I miss you some - how.
Nev - er thought it would end.
From the

Chorus:
G
D/F#
Em7
21 34
1 23
1 3
Cont. rhy. simile
bot - tom of my bro - ken heart there's just a thing or two I'd like you to know.

G/D
Cmaj7
Bm7
34
32
13121
You were my first love. You were my true love, from the first kiss -

Am7
C/D
G
2 1
2333
21 34
- es to the ver - y last rose. From the bot - tom of my bro - ken heart,

D/F#
Em7
G/D
1 23
1 3
34
e - ven though time may find me some-bod - y new. You were my real

Cmaj7
Bm7
Am7
To Coda
32
13121
2 1
love, I nev - er knew love till there was you. From the

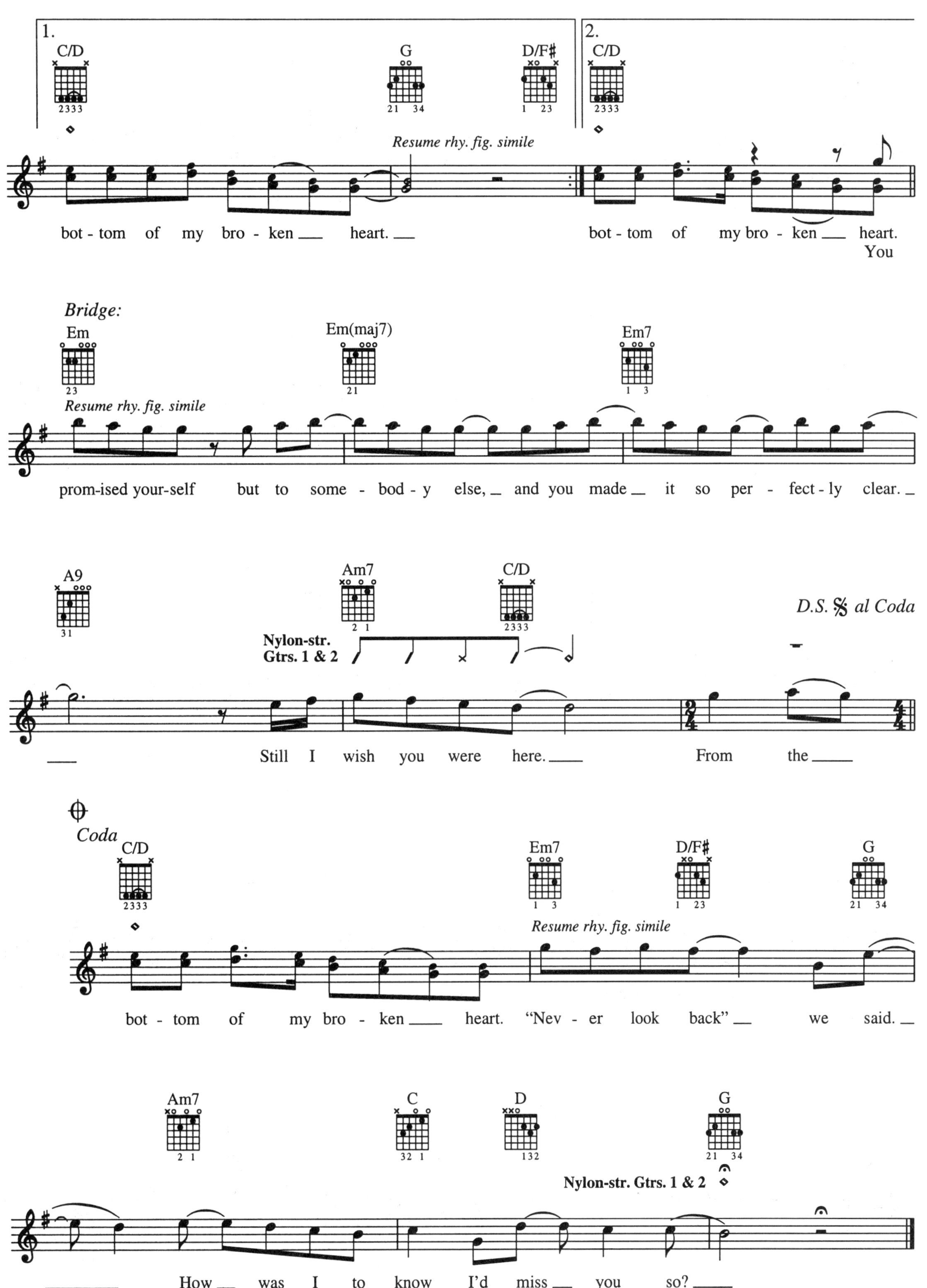
1.
C/D
G
D/F♯
2.
C/D
Resume rhy. fig. simile
bot - tom of my bro - ken heart.
bot - tom of my bro - ken heart.
You
Bridge:
Em
Em(maj7)
Em7
Resume rhy. fig. simile
prom-ised your-self but to some - bod - y else, and you made it so per - fect - ly clear.
A9
Am7
C/D
D.S. 𝄋 al Coda
Nylon-str. Gtrs. 1 & 2
Still I wish you were here.
From the
Coda
C/D
Em7
D/F♯
G
Resume rhy. fig. simile
bot - tom of my bro - ken heart. "Nev - er look back" we said.
Am7
C
D
G
Nylon-str. Gtrs. 1 & 2
How was I to know I'd miss you so?

GENIE IN A BOTTLE

Tune down 1/2 step:
⑥= E♭ ③= G♭
⑤= A♭ ②= B♭
④= D♭ ①= E♭

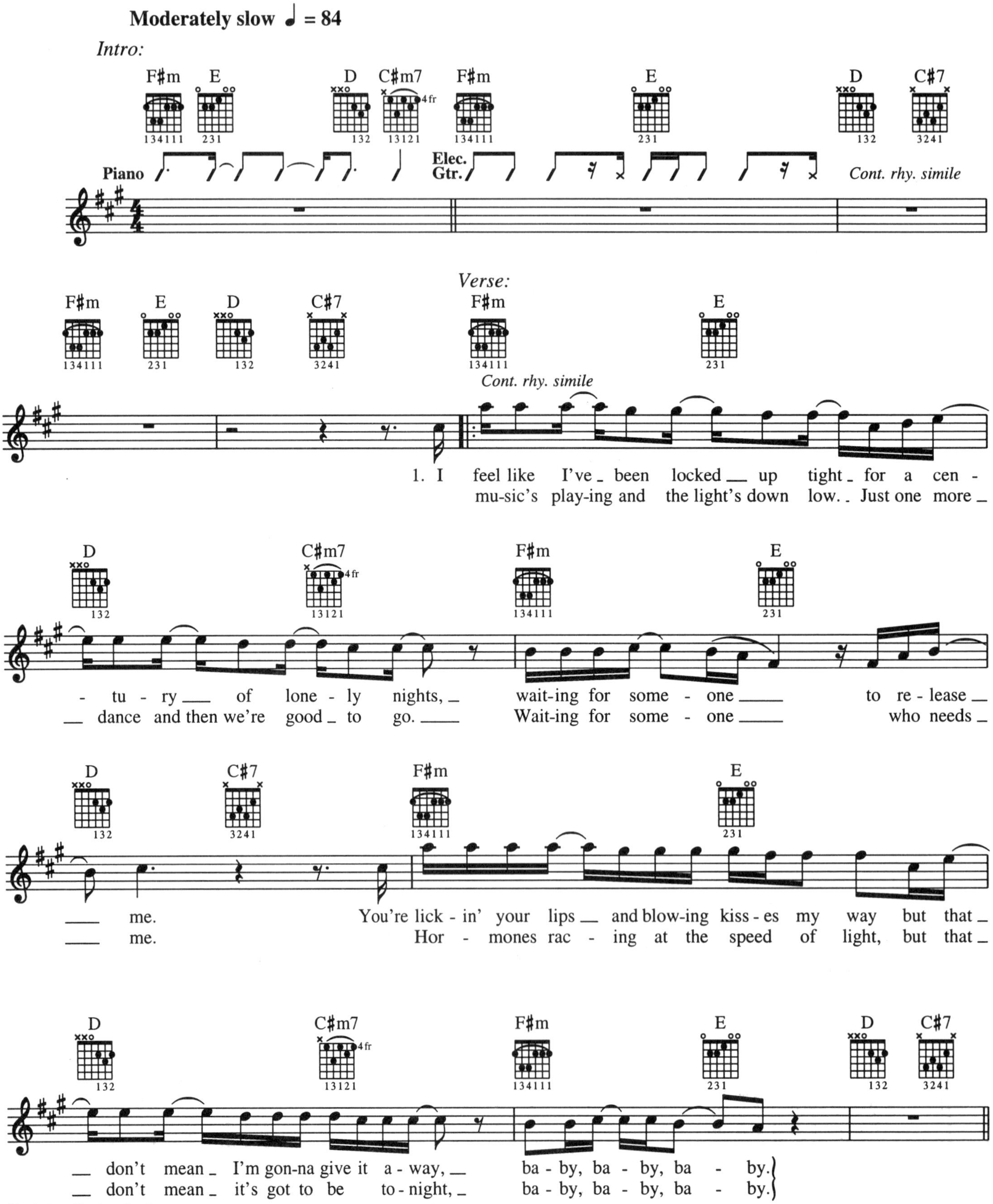

Words and Music by PAMELA SHEYNE, DAVID FRANK and STEVE KIPNER

Moderately slow ♩ = 84

Intro:

F♯m E D C♯m7 F♯m E D C♯7

Piano Elec. Gtr. *Cont. rhy. simile*

F♯m E D C♯7

Verse:

F♯m E

Cont. rhy. simile

1. I feel like I've been locked up tight for a cen-
music's play-ing and the light's down low. Just one more

D C♯m7 F♯m E

-tu-ry of lone-ly nights, wait-ing for some-one to re-lease
dance and then we're good to go. Wait-ing for some-one who needs

D C♯7 F♯m E

me. You're lick-in' your lips and blow-ing kiss-es my way but that
me. Hor-mones rac-ing at the speed of light, but that

D C♯m7 F♯m E D C♯7

don't mean I'm gon-na give it a-way, ba-by, ba-by, ba-by.
don't mean it's got to be to-night, ba-by, ba-by, ba-by.

Genie in a Bottle – 3 – 1
GFM0012

Pre-chorus:
F♯m E D C♯m7 F♯m E
Cont. rhy. simile
Oh, my bod-y's say-ing, "Let's go?" Oh,
Chorus:
D C♯m7 F♯m E D C♯m7
Cont. rhy. simile
but my heart is say-ing, "No." If you want to be with me, ba-by, there's a price to
F♯m E D C♯7 F♯m E
pay. I'm a ge-nie in a bot-tle, you got-ta rub me the right way. If you want to be with
D C♯m7 F♯m E
me, I can make your wish come true.
You got-ta make a big im-pres-
Just come and set me
To Coda
D C♯7 F♯m E
sion, I got-ta like what you do.
free, and, ba-by, I'll be with you.
I'm a ge-nie in a bot-tle, ba-by,
D C♯m7 F♯m E
you got-ta rub me the right way, hon-ey. I'm a ge-nie in a bot-tle, ba-by,
1. D C♯7
come, come, come on and let me out.
2. The
2. D C♯7
come, come, come on and let me out.

F♯m
E
D
C♯m7
4fr
134111
231
132
13121
I'm a gen-ie in a bot - tle, ba - by, you got-ta rub me the right way, hon - ey.
D.S. 𝄋 al Coda
F♯m
E
D
C♯7
3241
I'm a ge-nie in a bot - tle, ba - by, come, come, come on and let me out.
Coda
If you want to be with me, ba - by, there's a price to pay. I'm a ge - nie in a bot-
tle, you got-ta rub me the right way. If you want to be with me, I can make your wish come
true. Just come and set me free, ba - by, and I'll be with you.
N.C.
Elec. Gtr.
I'm a ge - nie in a bot - tle, ba - by, come, come, come on and let me out.

(GOD MUST HAVE SPENT) A LITTLE MORE TIME ON YOU

Words and Music by
CAROL STURKEN and EVAN ROGERS

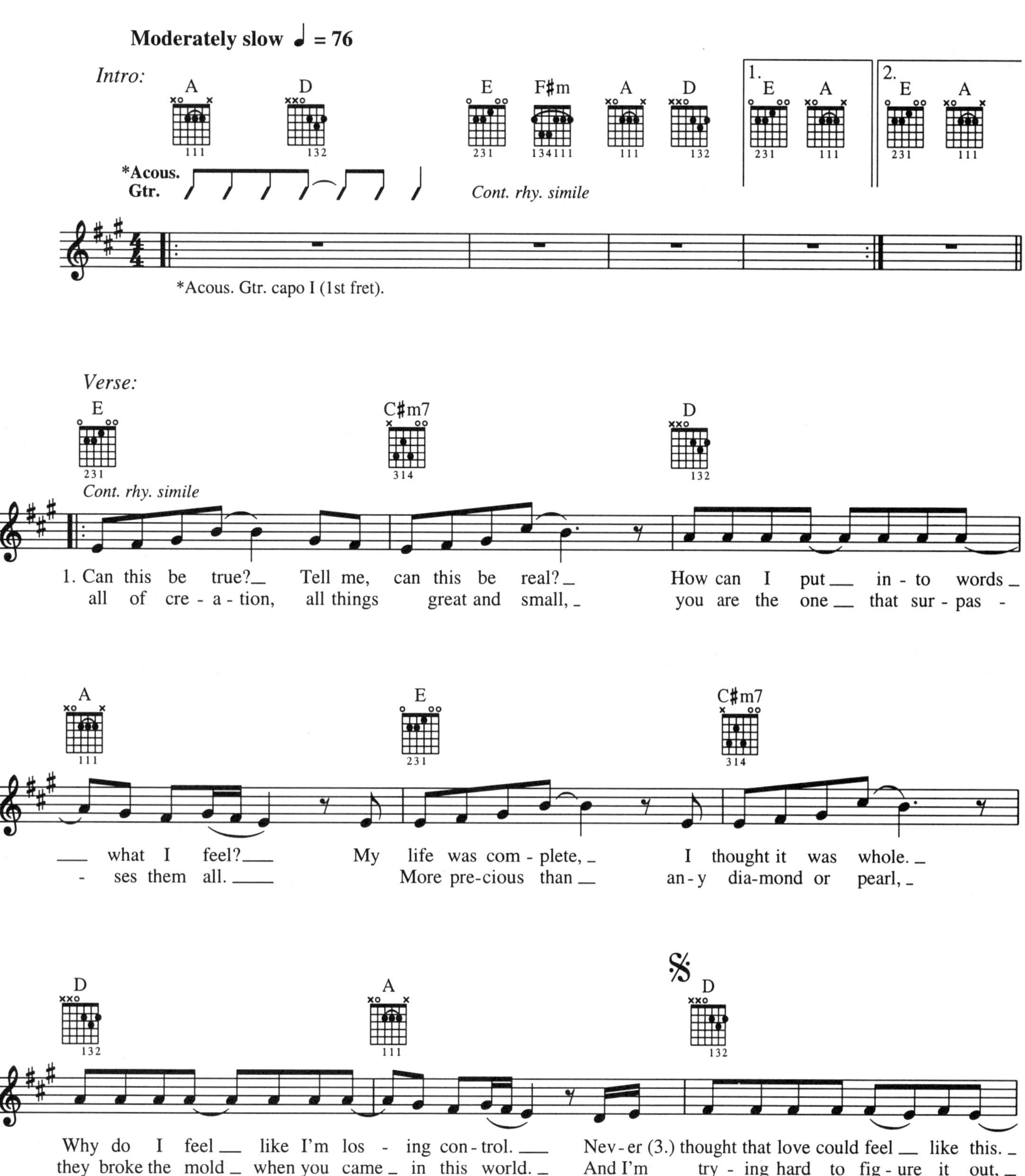
Moderately slow ♩ = 76
Intro:
A
D
E
F#m
A
D
1.
E
A
2.
E
A
*Acous. Gtr.
Cont. rhy. simile
*Acous. Gtr. capo I (1st fret).
Verse:
E
C#m7
D
Cont. rhy. simile
1. Can this be true? Tell me, can this be real? How can I put into words
all of cre-a-tion, all things great and small, you are the one that sur-pas-
A
E
C#m7
what I feel? My life was com-plete, I thought it was whole.
-ses them all. More pre-cious than an-y dia-mond or pearl,
D
A
D
Why do I feel like I'm los-ing con-trol. Nev-er (3.) thought that love could feel like this.
they broke the mold when you came in this world. And I'm try-ing hard to fig-ure it out,

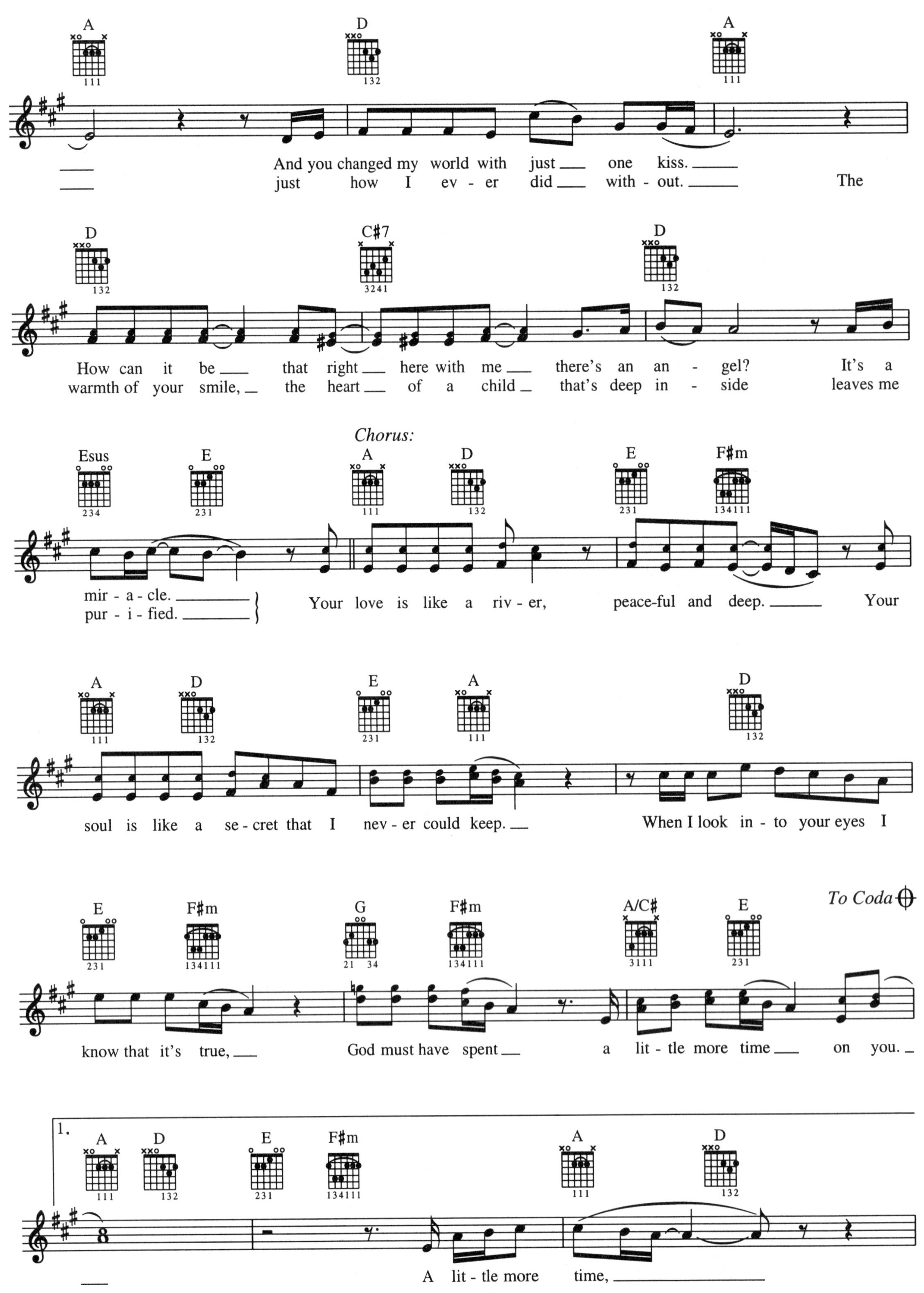
A
D
A
And you changed my world with just one kiss.
just how I ev - er did with - out. The
D
C#7
D
How can it be that right here with me there's an an - gel? It's a
warmth of your smile, the heart of a child that's deep in - side leaves me
Chorus:
Esus
E
A
D
E
F#m
mir - a - cle.
pur - i - fied.
Your love is like a riv - er, peace-ful and deep. Your
A
D
E
A
D
soul is like a se - cret that I nev - er could keep.
When I look in - to your eyes I
E
F#m
G
F#m
A/C#
E
To Coda
know that it's true, God must have spent a lit - tle more time on you.
1.
A
D
E
F#m
A
D
A lit - tle more time,

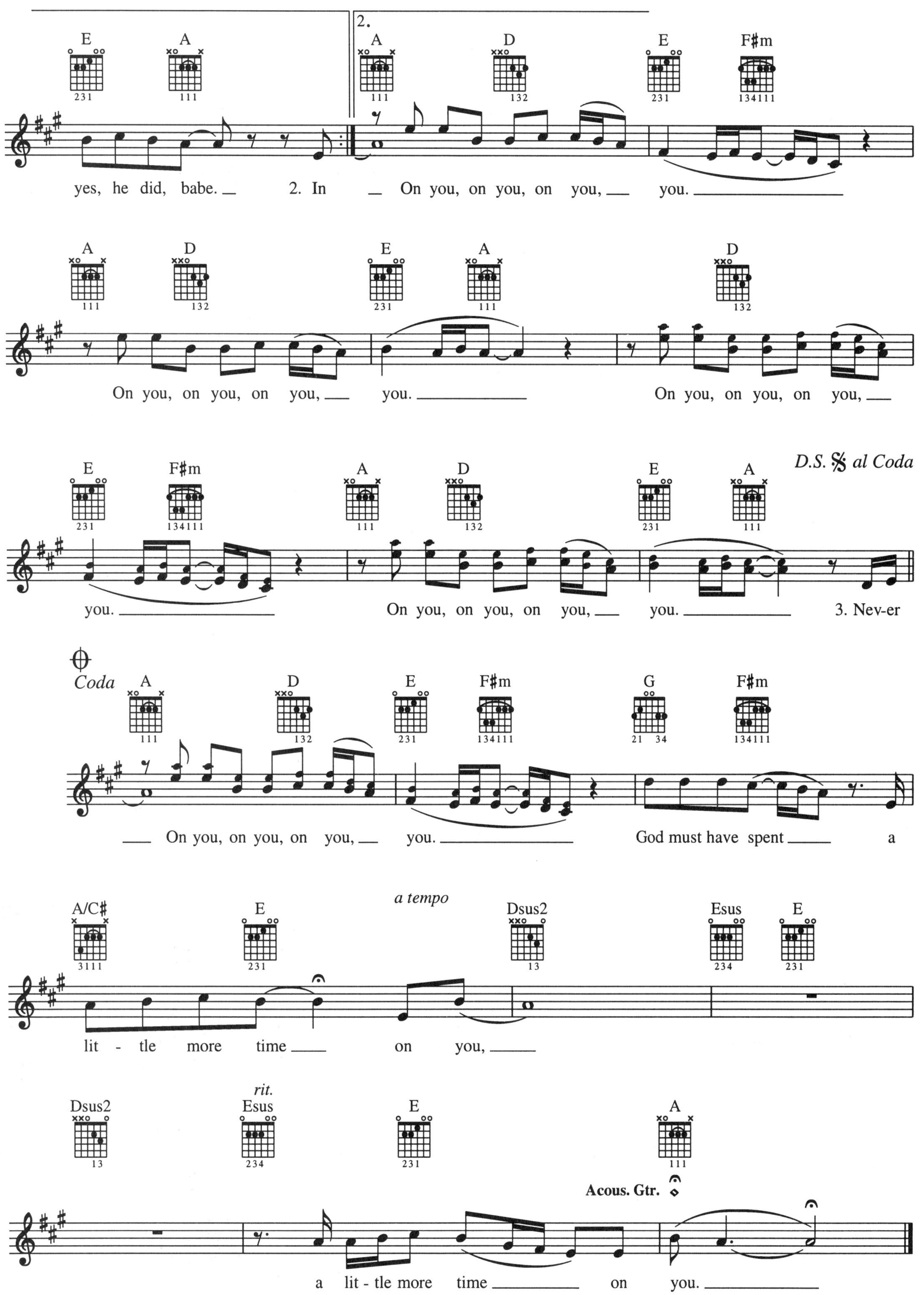
2.
E
A
A
D
E
F♯m
yes, he did, babe. 2. In On you, on you, on you, you.
On you, on you, on you, you.
On you, on you, on you,
D.S. 𝄋 al Coda
you. On you, on you, on you, you. 3. Nev-er
Coda
G
On you, on you, on you, you. God must have spent a
a tempo
A/C♯
Dsus2
Esus
lit - tle more time on you,
rit.
Acous. Gtr.
a lit - tle more time on you.

I DO (CHERISH YOU)

Words and Music by
KEITH STEGALL and DAN HILL

Tune down 1/2 step:
⑥= E♭ ③= G♭
⑤= A♭ ②= B♭
④= D♭ ①= E♭

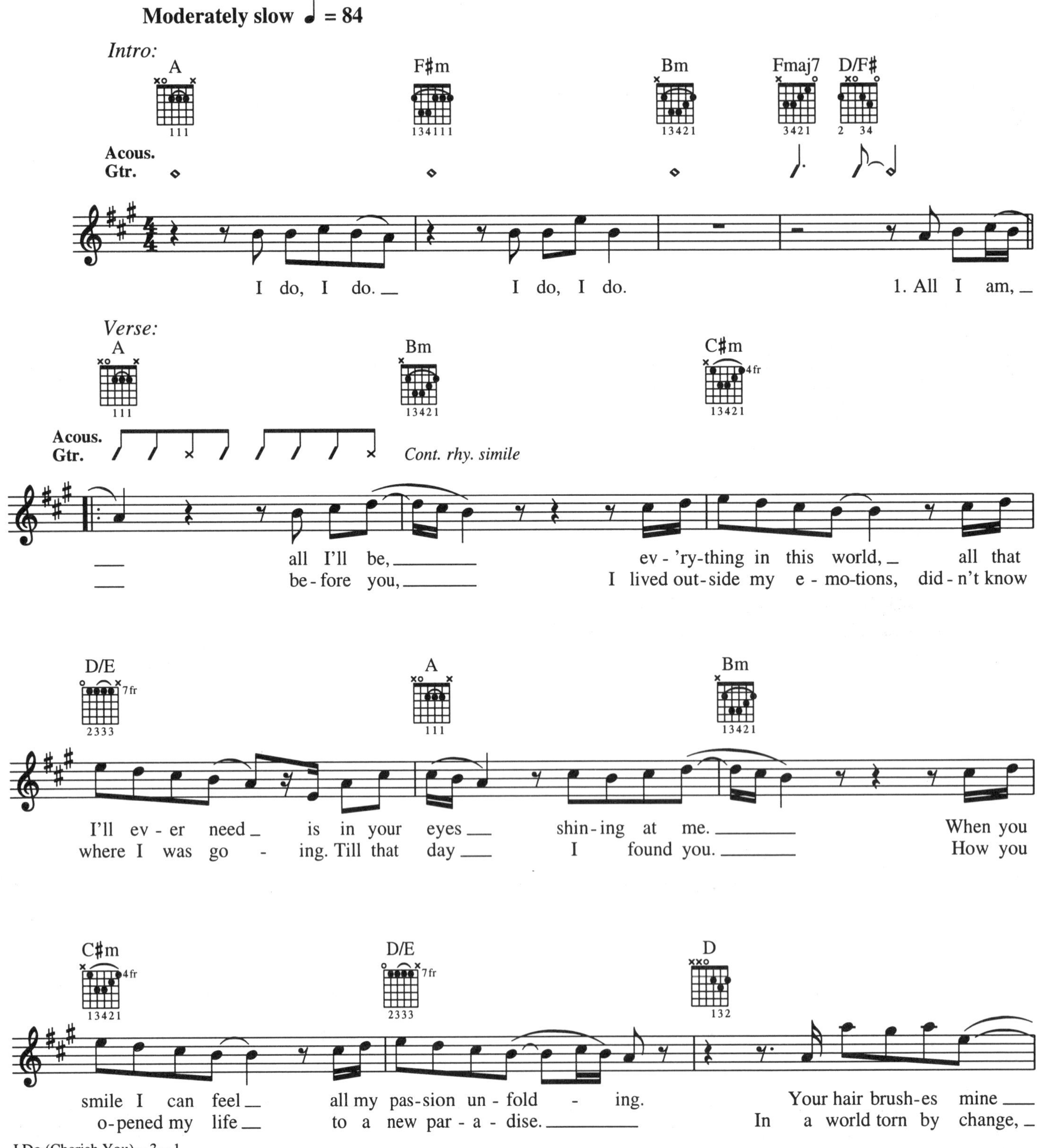

A/C♯
D
D/E
and a thou-sand sen - sa - tions se - duce me 'cause I...
still with all my heart, un - til my dy - ing day.
I do
Chorus:
A
F♯m
Bm
Cont. rhy. simile
cher - ish you for the rest of my life, you don't
D/E
A
F♯m
have to think twice. I will love you still from the
Bm
C♯7sus
C♯7
F♯m
E
depths of my soul, it's be - yond my con - trol. I've wait - ed so long to say this to you.
B9/D♯
Bm
1.
D/E
If you're ask - ing do I love you this much, I do.
A
F♯m
Bm
Oh, ba - by.

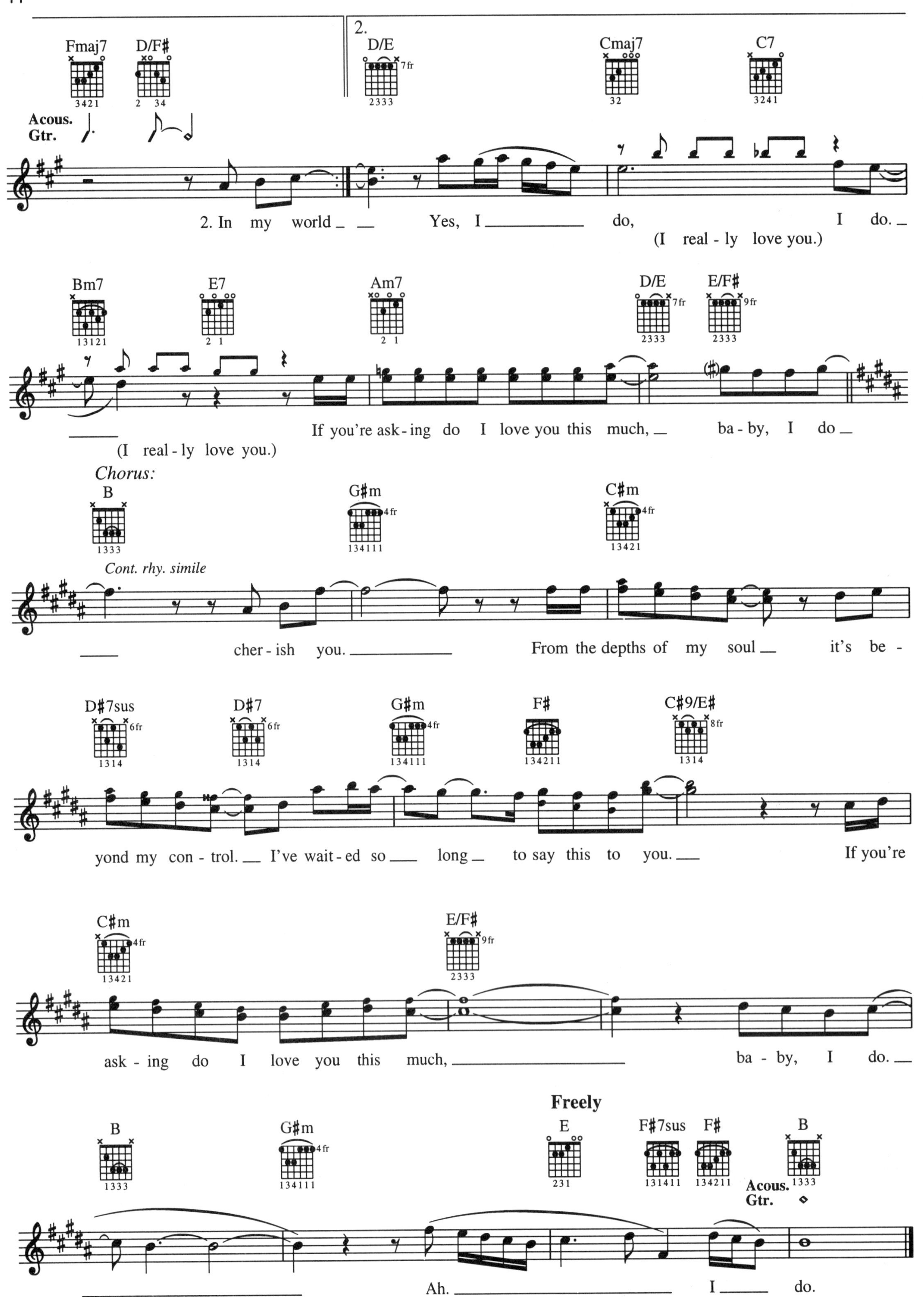

2.
Fmaj7
D/F♯
D/E
Cmaj7
C7
Acous. Gtr.
2. In my world
Yes, I
do,
I do.
(I really love you.)
Bm7
E7
Am7
D/E
E/F♯
If you're asking do I love you this much,
baby, I do
(I really love you.)
Chorus:
B
G♯m
C♯m
Cont. rhy. simile
cherish you.
From the depths of my soul
it's beyond my control.
D♯7sus
D♯7
G♯m
F♯
C♯9/E♯
I've waited so long
to say this to you.
If you're
C♯m
E/F♯
asking do I love you this much,
baby, I do.
Freely
B
G♯m
E
F♯7sus
F♯
B
Acous. Gtr.
Ah.
I
do.

SOMETIMES

Words and Music by
JÖRGEN ELOFSSON

All Gtrs. capo I (1st fret)
Moderately slow ♩ = 96
Intro:
A
E/G♯
F♯m
Bm7
E7sus
Acous. Gtr.
Riff A
end Riff A
mf
Verse:
A
A/C♯
E/G♯
E
Bm7
Elec. Gtr.
Cont. rhy. simile
1. You tell me you're in love with me, like you can't take your pret - ty eyes a - way from me. It's not that I don't want to stay, but ev - 'ry time you come too close, I move a - way.
2. I don't wan - na be so shy. Ev - 'ry time that I'm a - lone I won - der why. Hope that you will wait for me. You'll see that you're the on - ly one for me.
E7sus
I wan - na be - lieve in ev - 'ry-thing that you say, 'cause it sounds so good. But

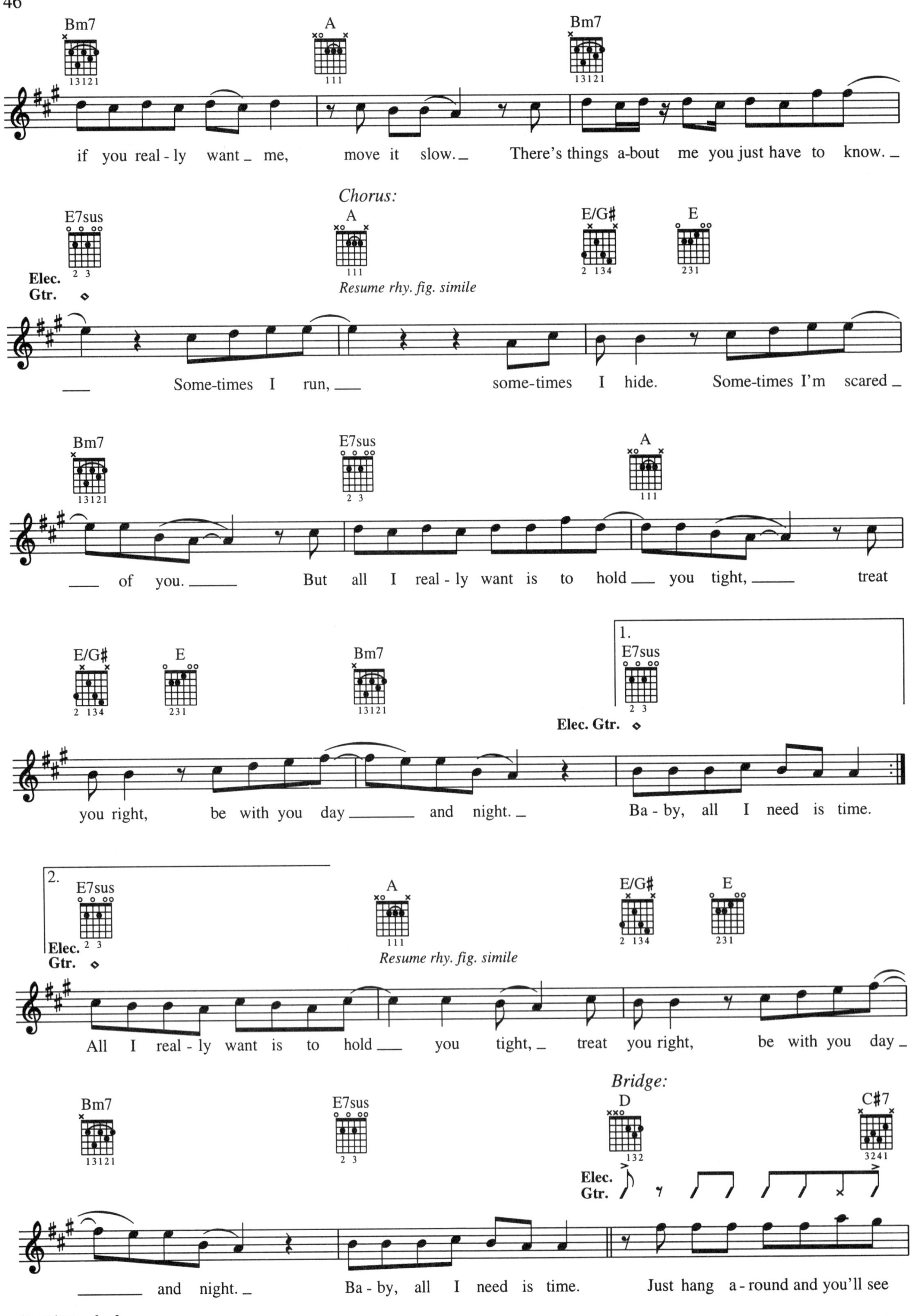
Bm7 A Bm7
if you real - ly want _ me, move it slow. _ There's things a-bout me you just have to know. _
Chorus:
E7sus A E/G♯ E
Elec. Gtr.
Resume rhy. fig. simile
___ Some-times I run, ___ some-times I hide. Some-times I'm scared _
Bm7 E7sus A
___ of you. ______ But all I real - ly want is to hold ___ you tight, ______ treat
E/G♯ E Bm7
1. E7sus
Elec. Gtr.
you right, be with you day ________ and night. _ Ba - by, all I need is time.
2. E7sus A E/G♯ E
Elec. Gtr.
Resume rhy. fig. simile
All I real - ly want is to hold ___ you tight, _ treat you right, be with you day _
Bm7 E7sus
Bridge:
D C♯7
Elec. Gtr.
________ and night. _ Ba - by, all I need is time. Just hang a - round and you'll see

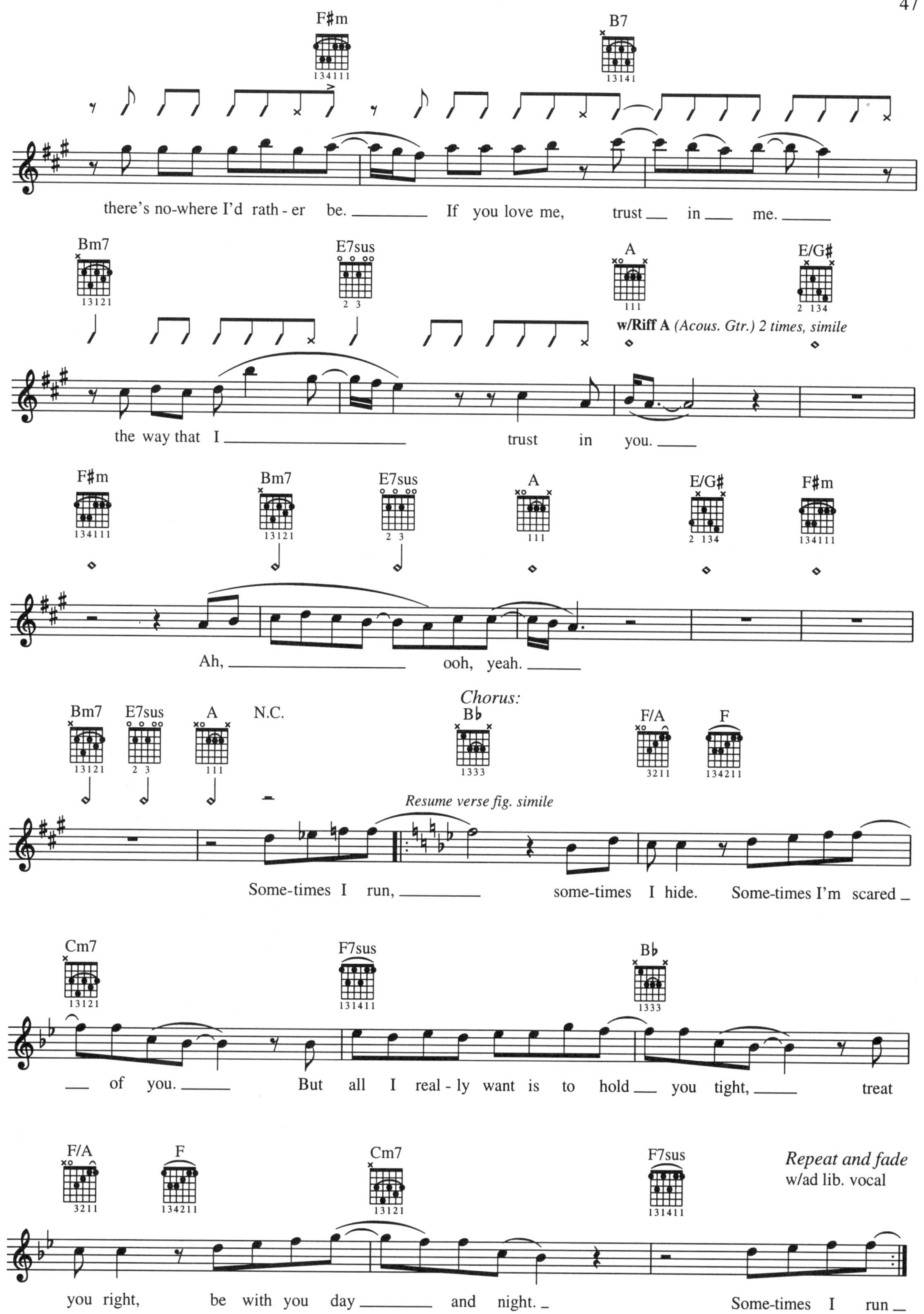
F♯m
B7
there's no-where I'd rath - er be. If you love me, trust in me.
Bm7
E7sus
A
E/G♯
w/Riff A (Acous. Gtr.) 2 times, simile
the way that I trust in you.
F♯m
Bm7
E7sus
A
E/G♯
F♯m
Ah, ooh, yeah.
Bm7
E7sus
A
N.C.
Chorus:
B♭
F/A
F
Resume verse fig. simile
Some-times I run, some-times I hide. Some-times I'm scared
Cm7
F7sus
B♭
of you. But all I real - ly want is to hold you tight, treat
F/A
F
Cm7
F7sus
Repeat and fade
w/ad lib. vocal
you right, be with you day and night. Some-times I run

I MISS YOU SO MUCH

Words and Music by
DARYL SIMMONS and KENNY EDMONDES

Moderately slow ♩ = 82
Intro:
C
Fmaj7
C
*Acous. Gtr.
mf fingerstyle hold throughout
*Two gtrs. arr. for one.
Fmaj7
Dm
Am
Dm
C/E
Fmaj7
A♭maj7
Gm
C
Verse:
F
G
Am
F
G
Am
Acous. Gtr. cont. simile
1. I nev - er asked for this feel - ing. I nev - er thought I would fall.
2. What did I act like you mat - ter? It was sil - ly of me to be - lieve

F G Am G/B C
I nev - er knew how I felt till the day you were gone.
that if I just o - pened my heart, things would come nat - u - r'lly;

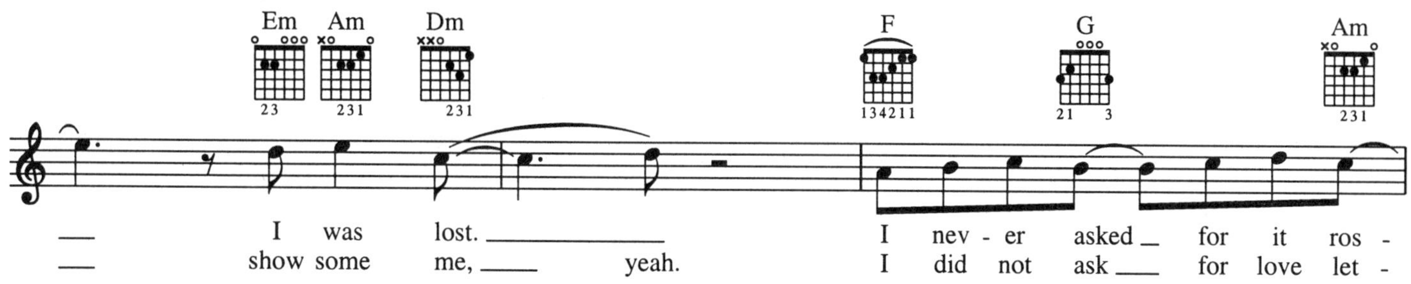
Em Am Dm F G Am
I was lost. I nev - er asked for it ros -
show some me, yeah. I did not ask for love let -

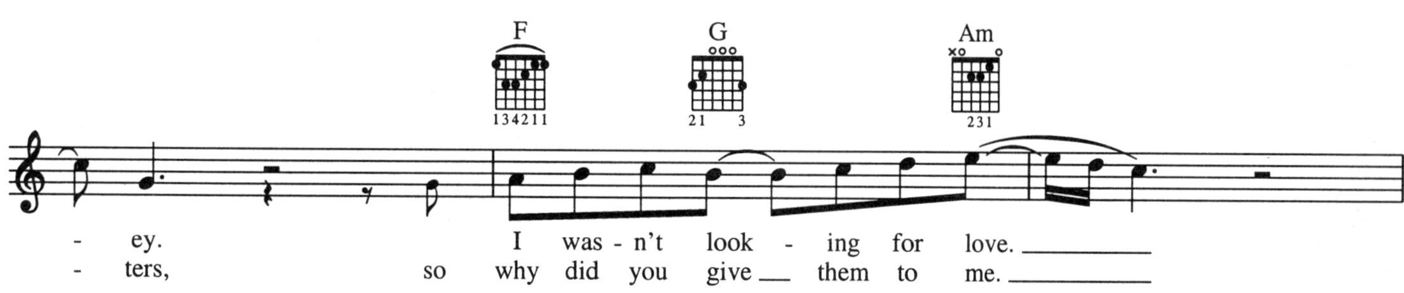
F G Am
- ey. I was - n't look - ing for love.
- ters, so why did you give them to me.

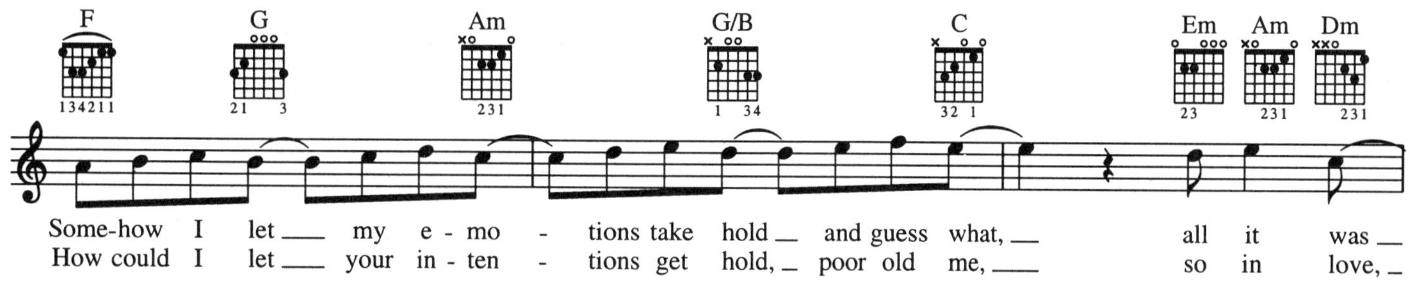
F G Am G/B C Em Am Dm
Some-how I let my e - mo - tions take hold and guess what, all it was
How could I let your in - ten - tions get hold, poor old me, so in love,

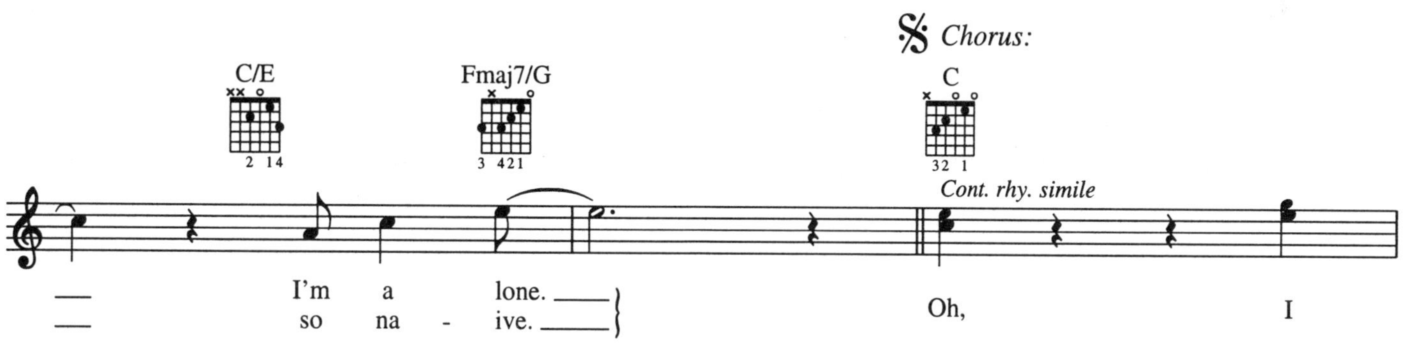
Chorus:
C/E Fmaj7/G C
Cont. rhy. simile
I'm a lone.
so na - ive.
Oh, I

Fmaj7
C
Fmaj7
miss you so much.
I long for your love.

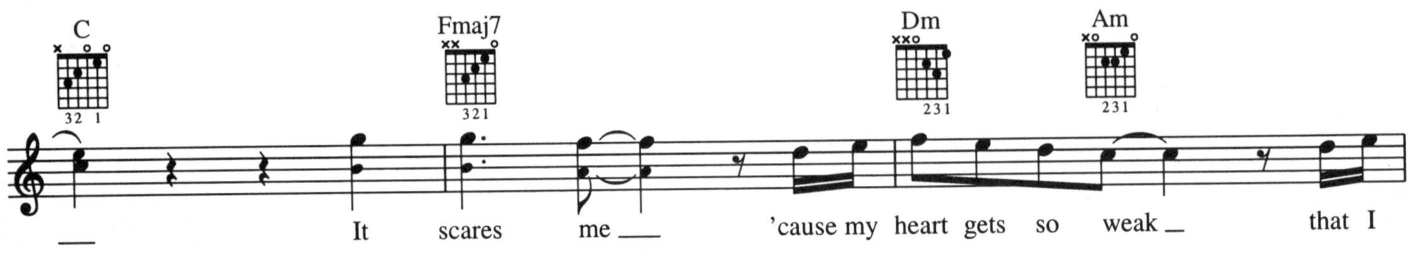
C
Fmaj7
Dm
Am
It scares me 'cause my heart gets so weak that I

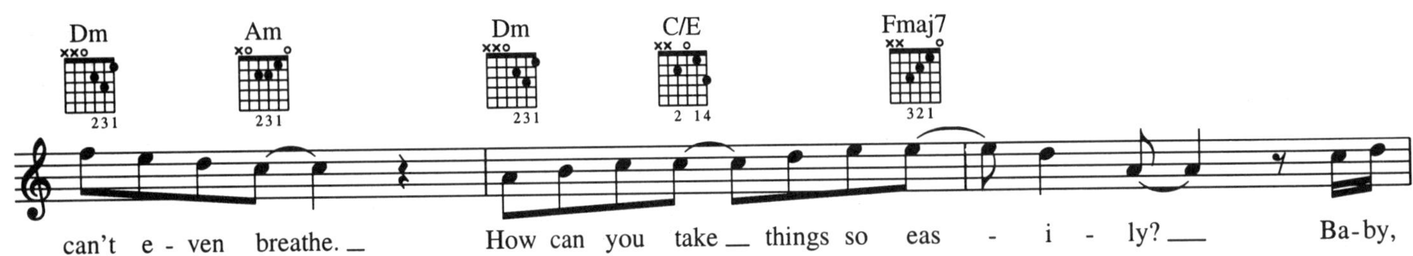
Dm
Am
Dm
C/E
Fmaj7
can't e - ven breathe. How can you take things so eas - i - ly? Ba-by,

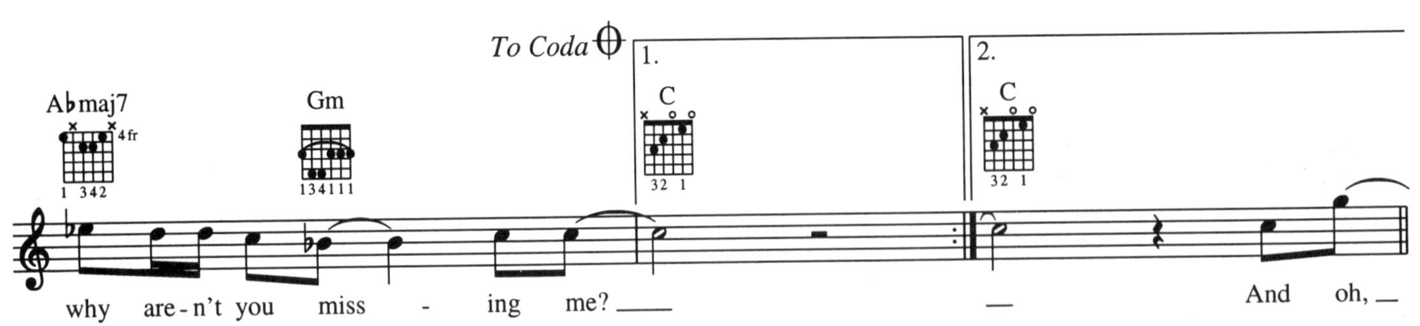
To Coda
1.
2.
Ab maj7
Gm
C
C
why are-n't you miss - ing me?
And oh,

Bridge:
Em
Fmaj7
Dm
F/G
Cont. rhy. simile
how I hate what you have done, made me fall

G/F
Em
Fmaj7
Em
Am
Dm
so deep in love.
God knows you're the on - ly one

C/E
Fmaj7/G
D.S. 𝄋 al Coda
I want, that I love. Oh, ba - by.

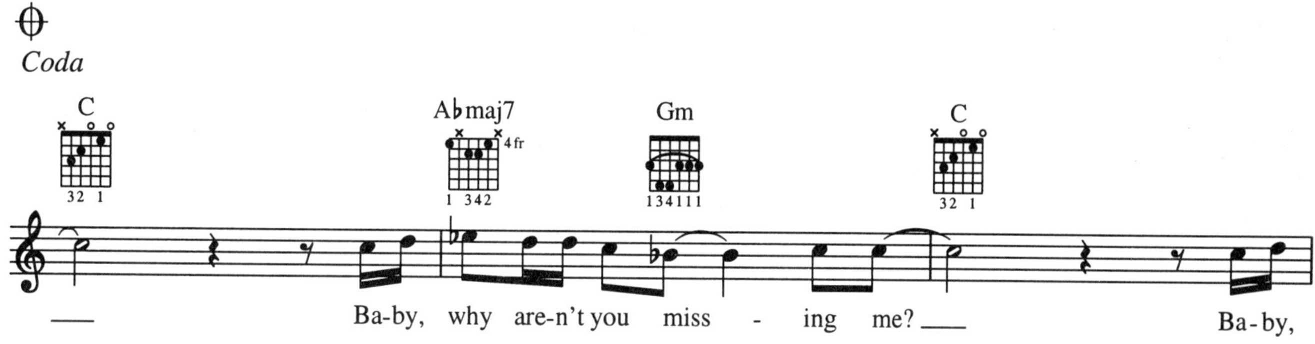
Coda
C
A♭maj7
Gm
C
Ba-by, why are-n't you miss - ing me? Ba-by,

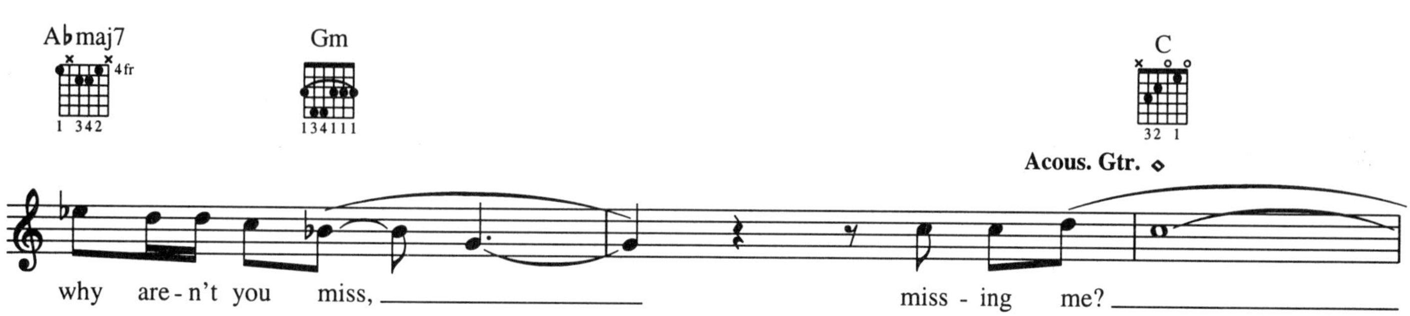
A♭maj7
Gm
C
Acous. Gtr.
why are-n't you miss, miss - ing me?

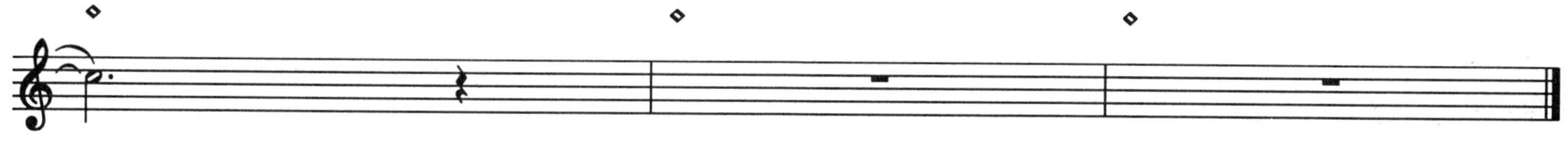

I WANT IT THAT WAY

Words and Music by MAX MARTIN
and ANDREAS CARLSSON

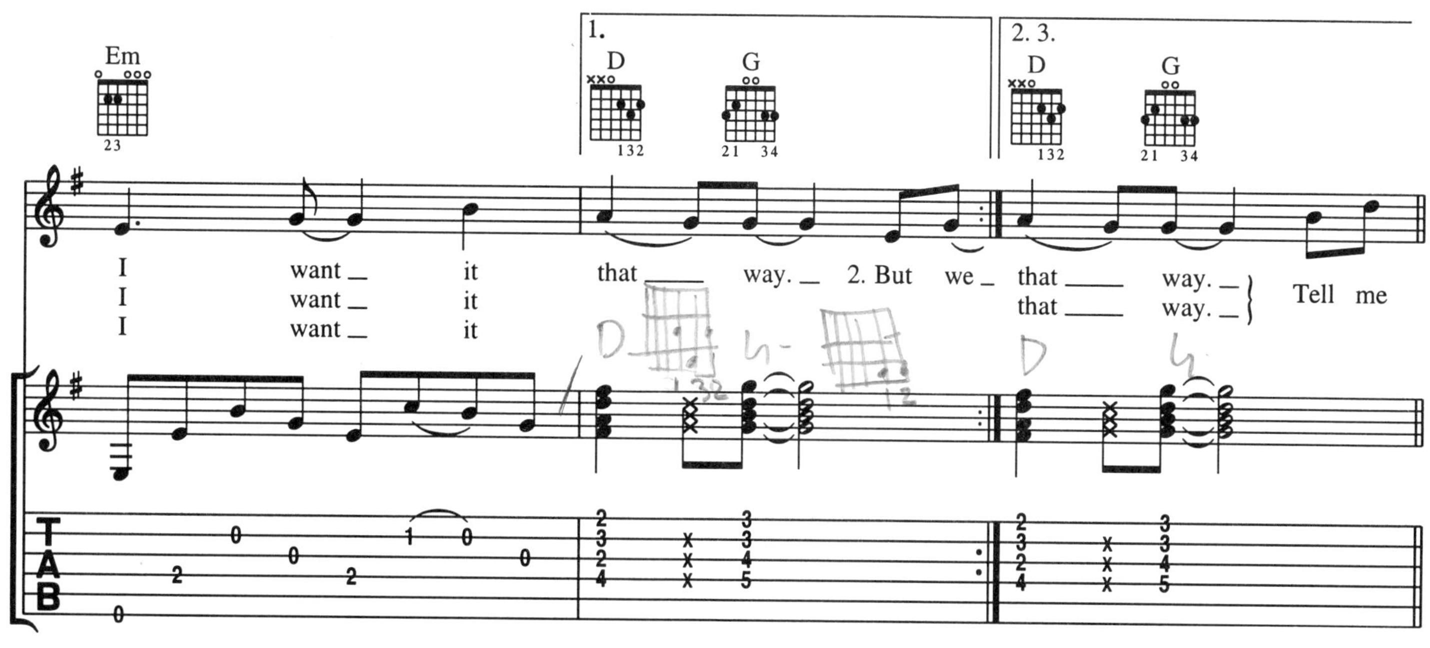
Em
1.
D
G
2. 3.
D
G
I want it that way. 2. But we that way. Tell me
I want it that way.
I want it
T
A
B

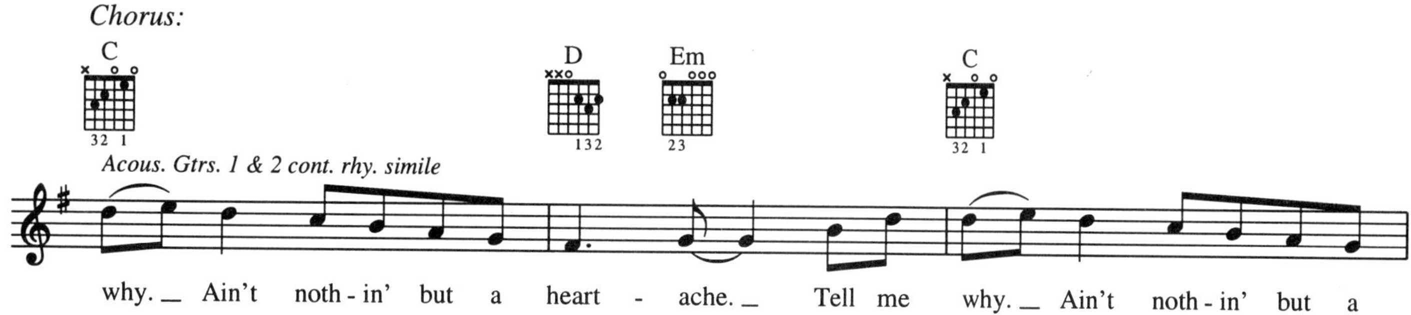
Chorus:
C
D
Em
C
Acous. Gtrs. 1 & 2 cont. rhy. simile
why. Ain't noth - in' but a heart - ache. Tell me why. Ain't noth - in' but a

D
Em
C
D
G
mis - take. Tell me why. I nev - er wan - na hear you say

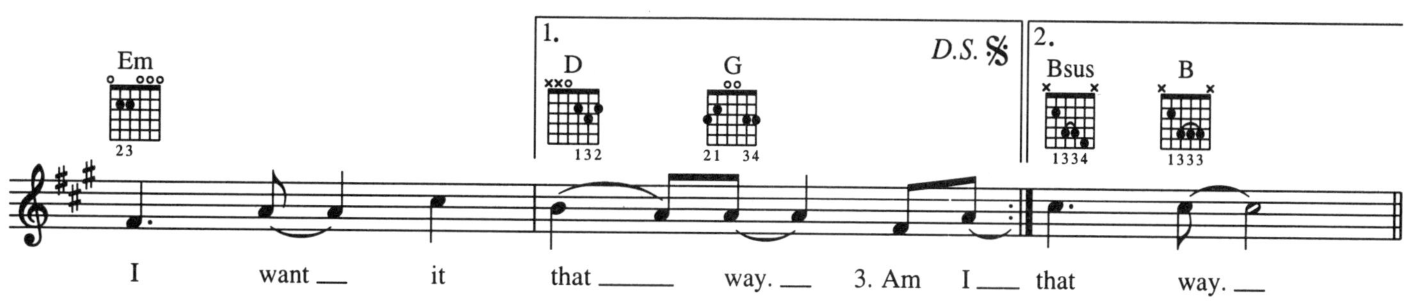
Em
1.
D
G
D.S.
2.
Bsus
B
I want it that way. 3. Am I that way.

Bridge:
Em
G
C
Cont. rhy. simile
Now I can see that we've fall - en a - part from the way that it used to be,
Am
D
Em
G
yeah. No mat - ter the dis - tance, I want you to know that
C
Dsus
D
C
Acous. Gtrs. 1 & 2
deep down in - side of me you are my
D
Em
C
D
Em
fi - re, the one de - si - re. You are,
C
D
G
Em
you are, you are, you are.

Am
D
E
F♯m
Resume rhy. fig. simile
Don't wan - na hear you say...
Ain't noth - in' but a heart - ache.
Ain't noth - in' but a mis - take.
I nev - er wan - na hear you say.
I want it that way.
Tell me
Chorus:
Cont. rhy. simile
why. Ain't noth - in' but a heart - ache. Tell me why. Ain't noth - in' but a mis - take. Tell me why. I nev - er wan - na hear you say.
I want it
1.
that way. Tell me
2.
that way. 'Cause I want it that way.
rit.
Acous. Gtrs. 1 & 2

I WILL BE THERE

Words and Music by
ANDREAS CARLSSON and MAX MARTIN

Tune down 1/2 step:
⑥= E♭ ③= G♭
⑤= A♭ ②= B♭
④= D♭ ①= E♭

Moderately ♩ = 96

Intro:

C♯m A B

Acous. Gtr. *Cont. rhy. simile*

f

A E Bsus B

Oh, ___ yeah. ___

Elec. Gtr.

Riff A

mf *w/slide*

G♯m C♯m A E

Acous. Gtr.

1. You don't have to say what's

end Riff A

I Will Be There – 4 – 1
GFM0012

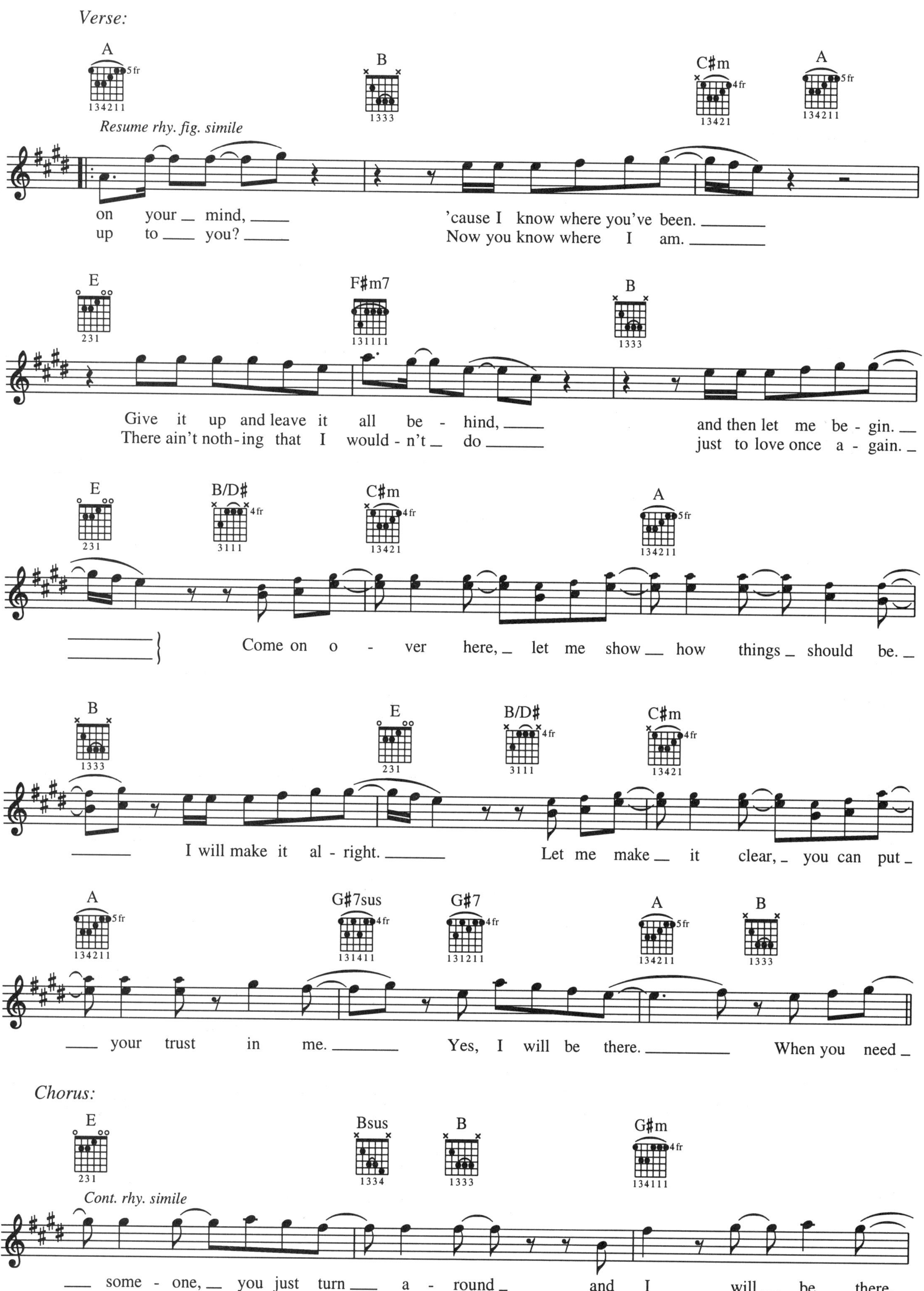
Verse:
A B C#m A
Resume rhy. fig. simile
on your mind, 'cause I know where you've been.
up to you? Now you know where I am.
E F#m7 B
Give it up and leave it all be - hind, and then let me be - gin.
There ain't noth - ing that I would - n't do just to love once a - gain.
E B/D# C#m A
Come on o - ver here, let me show how things should be.
B E B/D# C#m
I will make it al - right. Let me make it clear, you can put
A G#7sus G#7 A B
your trust in me. Yes, I will be there. When you need
Chorus:
E Bsus B G#m
Cont. rhy. simile
some - one, you just turn a - round and I will be there.

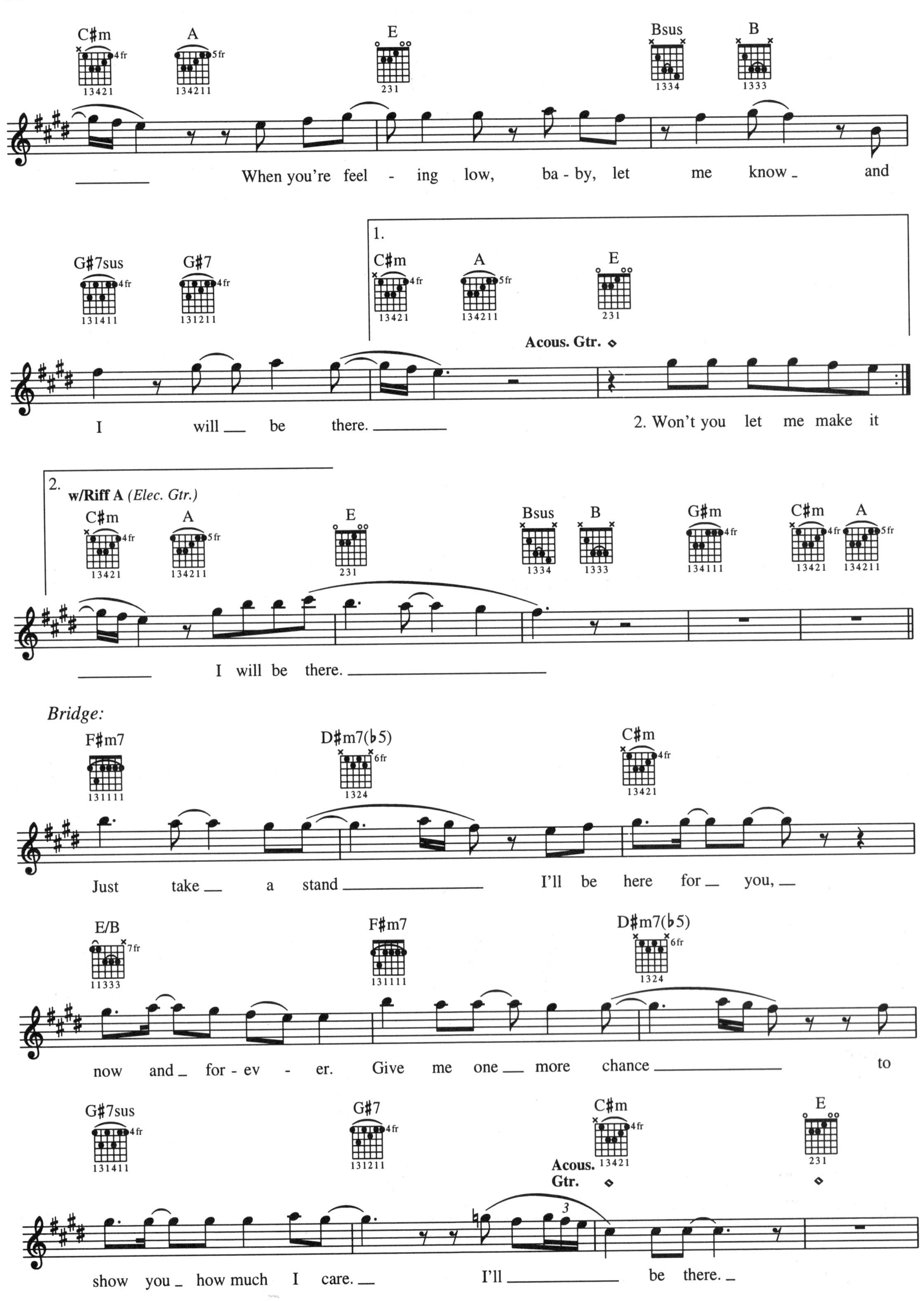

C♯m
A
E
Bsus
B
When you're feel - ing low, ba - by, let me know and
G♯7sus
G♯7
1.
C♯m
A
E
Acous. Gtr.
I will be there.
2. Won't you let me make it
2. w/Riff A (Elec. Gtr.)
C♯m
A
E
Bsus
B
G♯m
C♯m
A
I will be there.
Bridge:
F♯m7
D♯m7(♭5)
C♯m
Just take a stand
I'll be here for you,
E/B
F♯m7
D♯m7(♭5)
now and for - ev - er. Give me one more chance to
G♯7sus
G♯7
C♯m
E
Acous. Gtr.
show you how much I care.
I'll be there.

Mid-chorus:
B
A
B
E
Bsus
B
Resume rhy. fig. simile
When you need some - one,
G♯m
C♯m
A
E
Bsus
B
just turn a - round and I will be there.
When you're in sor - row,
Chorus:
G♯m
C♯m
A
E
Cont. rhy. simile
just let me know and I will be there.
1. When you need some - one, you just turn
2. Vocal ad lib.
Bsus
B
G♯m
C♯m
A
a - round and I will be there.
When you're feel -
E
Bsus
B
G♯7sus
G♯7
- ing low, ba - by, let me know and I will be there.
1.
w/Riff A (Elec. Gtr.) 2 times, simile
C♯m
A
(I will be there.)
2.
C♯m
A
E
Acous. Gtr.
(I will be there.)

IF SHE ONLY KNEW

Words and Music by
CRIS FARREN and GORDON CHAMBERS

Moderately ♩ = 96

Verses 1, 2, & 3:
E
C♯m7
A(9)
Acous. Gtr.
Cont. rhy. simile
what I knew but could - n't say.
what I feel here in my heart,
what I see when I close my eyes.
F♯m11
E
C♯m7
If she could just see the part of me that I hid a - way.
she'd know it was real, pure and true right from the start.
All that I dream so that she would re - al -
A(9)
F♯m11
C(9)
Oh, yeah. If I could just hold her in my arms
Oh, yeah. But I'm just a man who did - n't un -
ize. Uh, huh. But like a fool I wait - ed much
B7sus
B7
E
C♯m7
a - gain and just say, "I love you."
- der - stand what she was go - ing through.
too long to let her know the truth.
But she's gone a - way,
F♯m11
B7sus
E
Esus
may - be she'd stay if she on - ly knew.

1.
E
231
Acous. Gtr.
2.
E
231
3.
E
231
To Next Strain
(To Chorus:)
2. If she could just feel
And
Won't you tell me, tell me

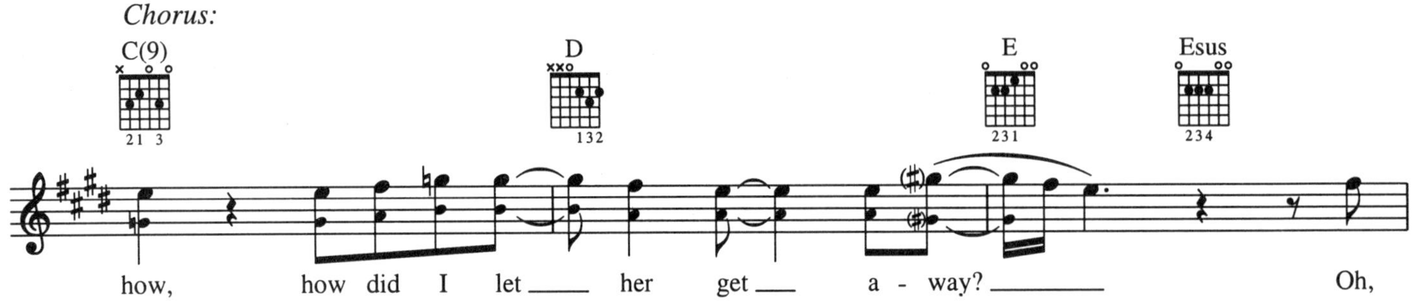
Chorus:
C(9)
21 3
D
132
E
231
Esus
234
how, how did I let her get a - way?
Oh,

E
231
C(9)
21 3
D
132
yeah, yeah, yeah. 'Cause love, love is so eas - y to feel. but the

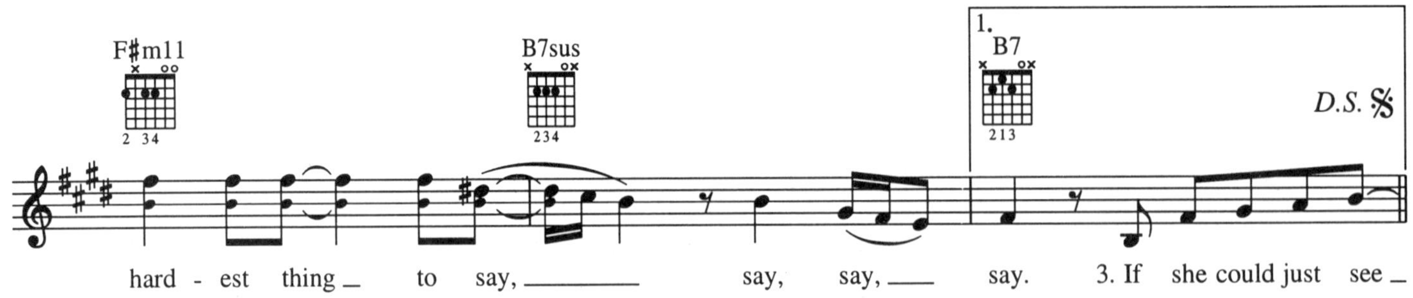
F♯m11
2 34
B7sus
234
1.
B7
213
D.S. 𝄋
hard - est thing to say, say, say, say. 3. If she could just see

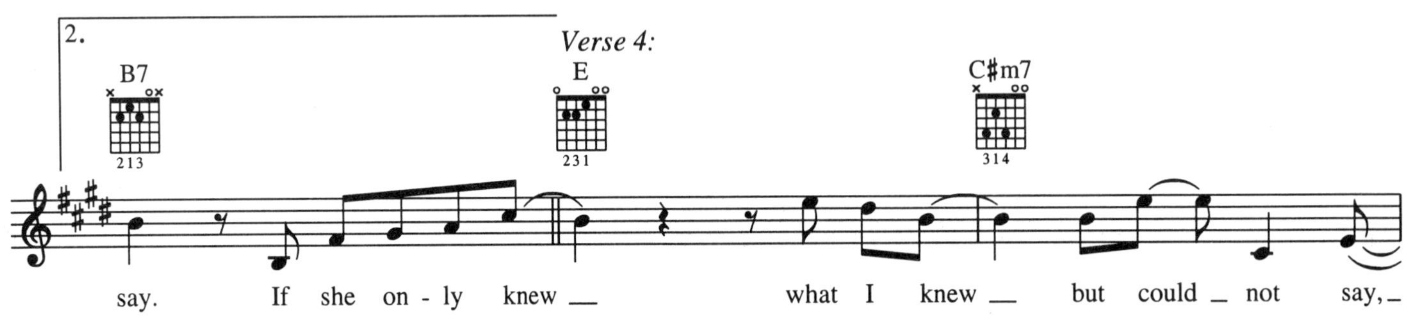
2.
B7
213
Verse 4:
E
231
C♯m7
314
say. If she on - ly knew what I knew but could not say,

A(9)
F♯m11
E
say, ba-by. If she could just see the part of me
C♯m7
A(9)
F♯m11
that I hid a - way. If I could just hold
C(9)
B7sus
B7
E
her in my arms a - gain and just say, "I love you."
C♯m7
F♯m11
"I love you." She's gone a - way, may - be she'd stay
Outro: w/ad lib. vocal
B7sus
B7
C(9)
if she on - ly knew. La - la - la - la - la -
D
E
Esus
E
Repeat and fade
- la - la - la - la.

IT'S GONNA BE ME

Words and Music by
MAX MARTIN, RAMI and ANDREAS CARLSSON

Cm
Gm/B♭
Gm
A♭
Gm
I re-mem-ber you told me that it made you be-lieve in
too blind to see, but in the end you know it's gon-na be me.
Fm7
B♭
Cm
B♭
no man, no cry. May - be that's why
You can't de - ny, so just tell me why
ev - 'ry lit - tle
Chorus:
A♭
Fm
B♭
Gm
Cm/G
Cm
thing I do nev - er seems e - nough for you. You don't wan - na
A♭
G/B
Cm
B♭
lose it a - gain, but I'm not like them. Ba - by, when you
1.
A♭
Fm
B♭
B♭6
Cm
B♭/D
fi - nal - ly get to love some - bod - y, guess
A♭
G7
N.C.
B♭5
2.
G/B
Cm
B♭/D
what? It's gon-na be me.
love some - bod - y, guess

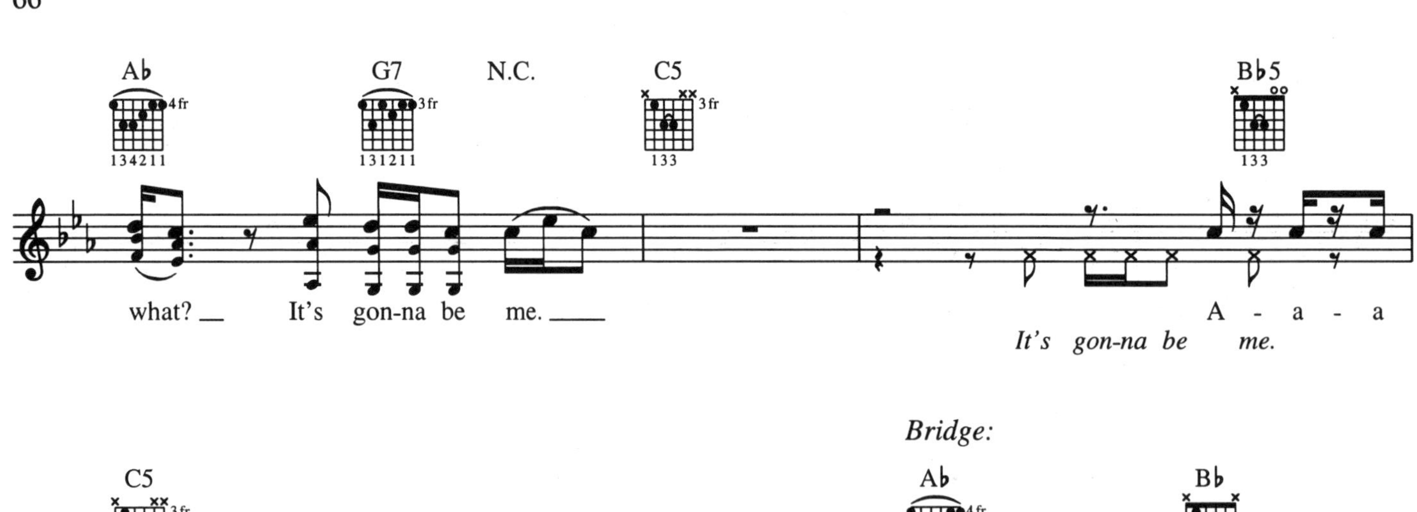
Ab
G7
N.C.
C5
Bb5
what? It's gon-na be me.
A - a - a
It's gon-na be me.

Bridge:
C5
Ab
Bb
ay. Ooh yeah yeah.
There comes a day when

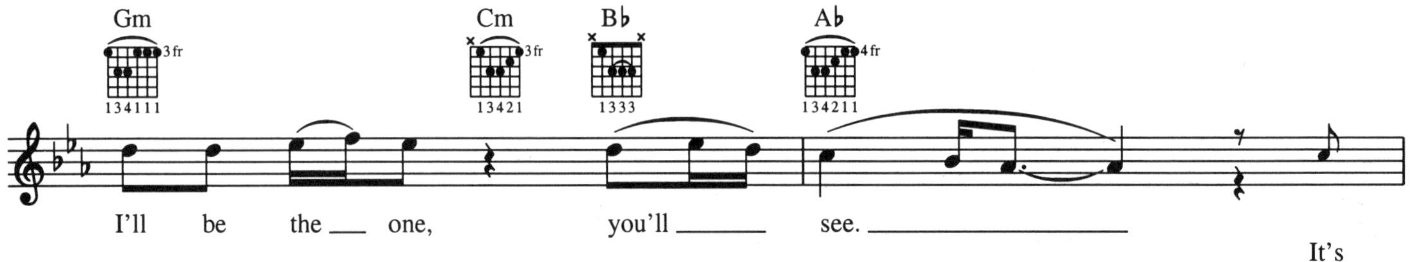
Gm
Cm
Bb
Ab
I'll be the one, you'll see.
It's

G7
N.C.
gon - na, gon - na, gon - na, gon - na, gon - na.
It's gon-na be me.

Interlude:

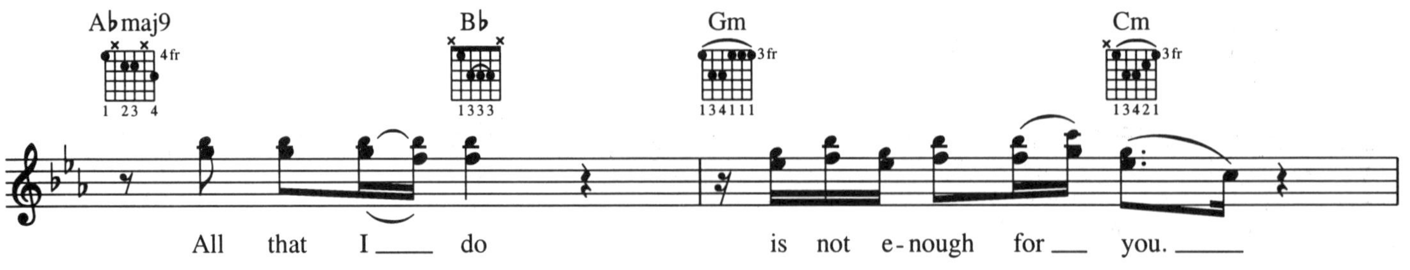
Abmaj9
Bb
Gm
Cm
All that I do is not e-nough for you.

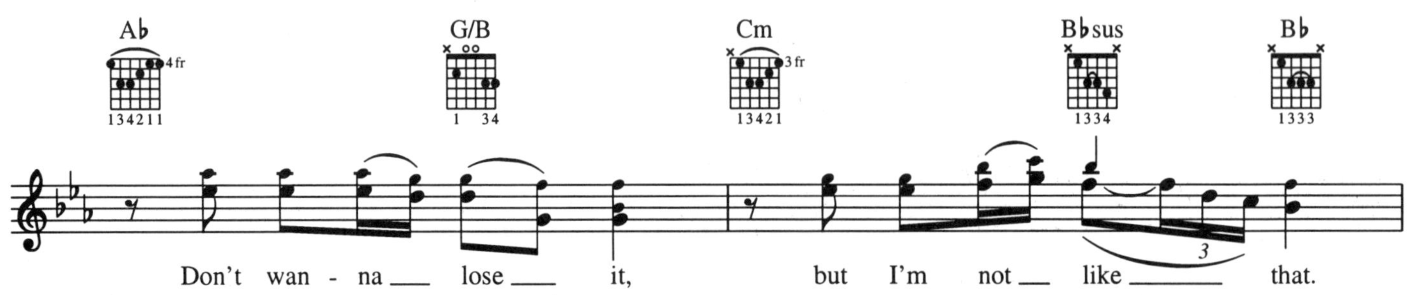
Ab
G/B
Cm
Bbsus
Bb
Don't wan - na lose it, but I'm not like that.

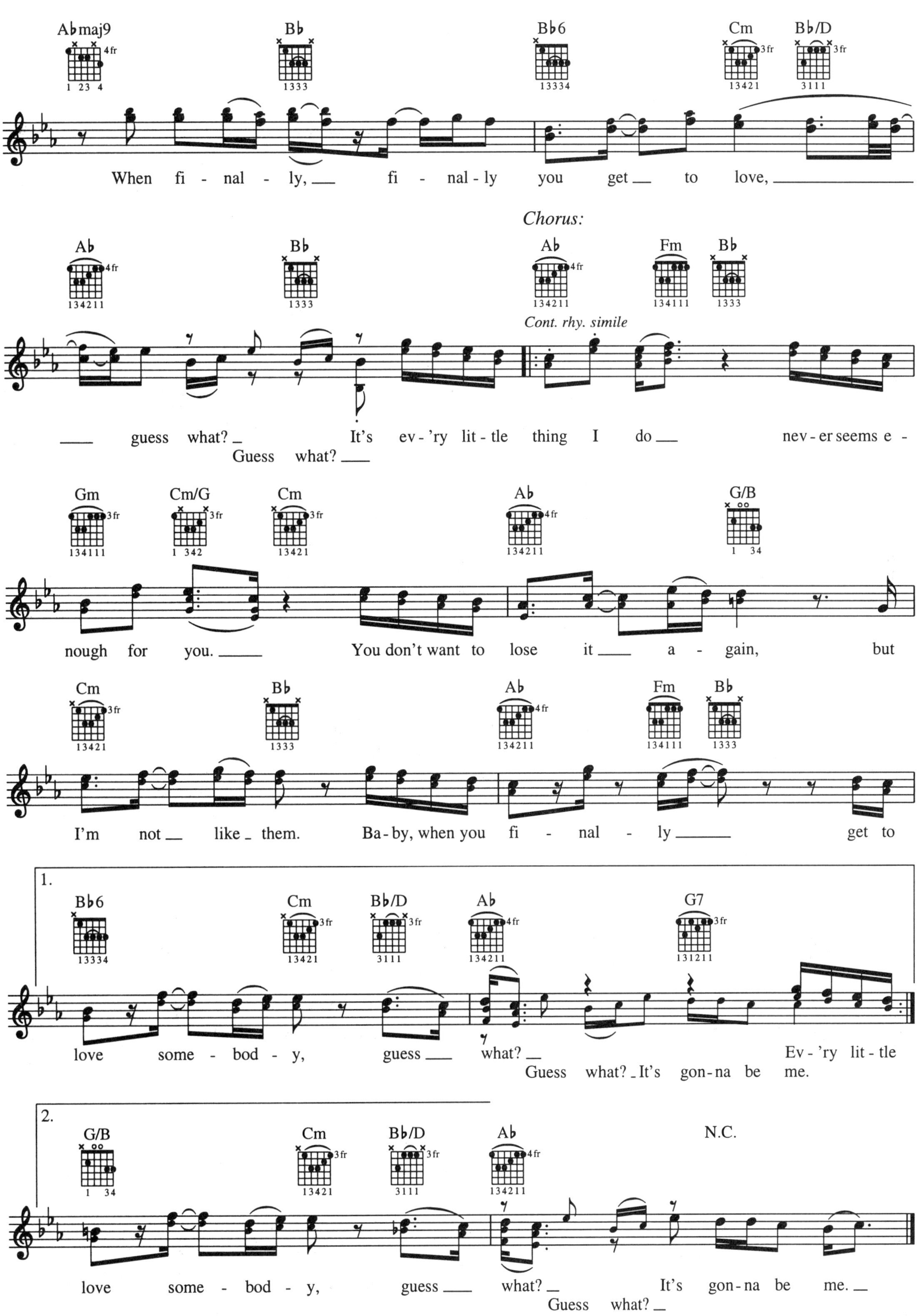

Abmaj9
Bb
Bb6
Cm
Bb/D
When fi - nal - ly, fi - nal - ly you get to love,
Chorus:
Ab
Bb
Ab
Fm
Bb
Cont. rhy. simile
guess what?
Guess what?
It's ev - 'ry lit - tle thing I do
nev - er seems e -
Gm
Cm/G
Cm
Ab
G/B
nough for you.
You don't want to lose it a - gain, but
Cm
Bb
Ab
Fm
Bb
I'm not like them.
Ba - by, when you fi - nal - ly get to
1.
Bb6
Cm
Bb/D
Ab
G7
love some - bod - y, guess what?
Guess what? It's gon - na be me.
Ev - 'ry lit - tle
2.
G/B
Cm
Bb/D
Ab
N.C.
love some - bod - y, guess what?
Guess what?
It's gon - na be me.

LARGER THAN LIFE

Words and Music by
MAX MARTIN, KRISTIAN LUNDIN
and BRIAN T. LITTRELL

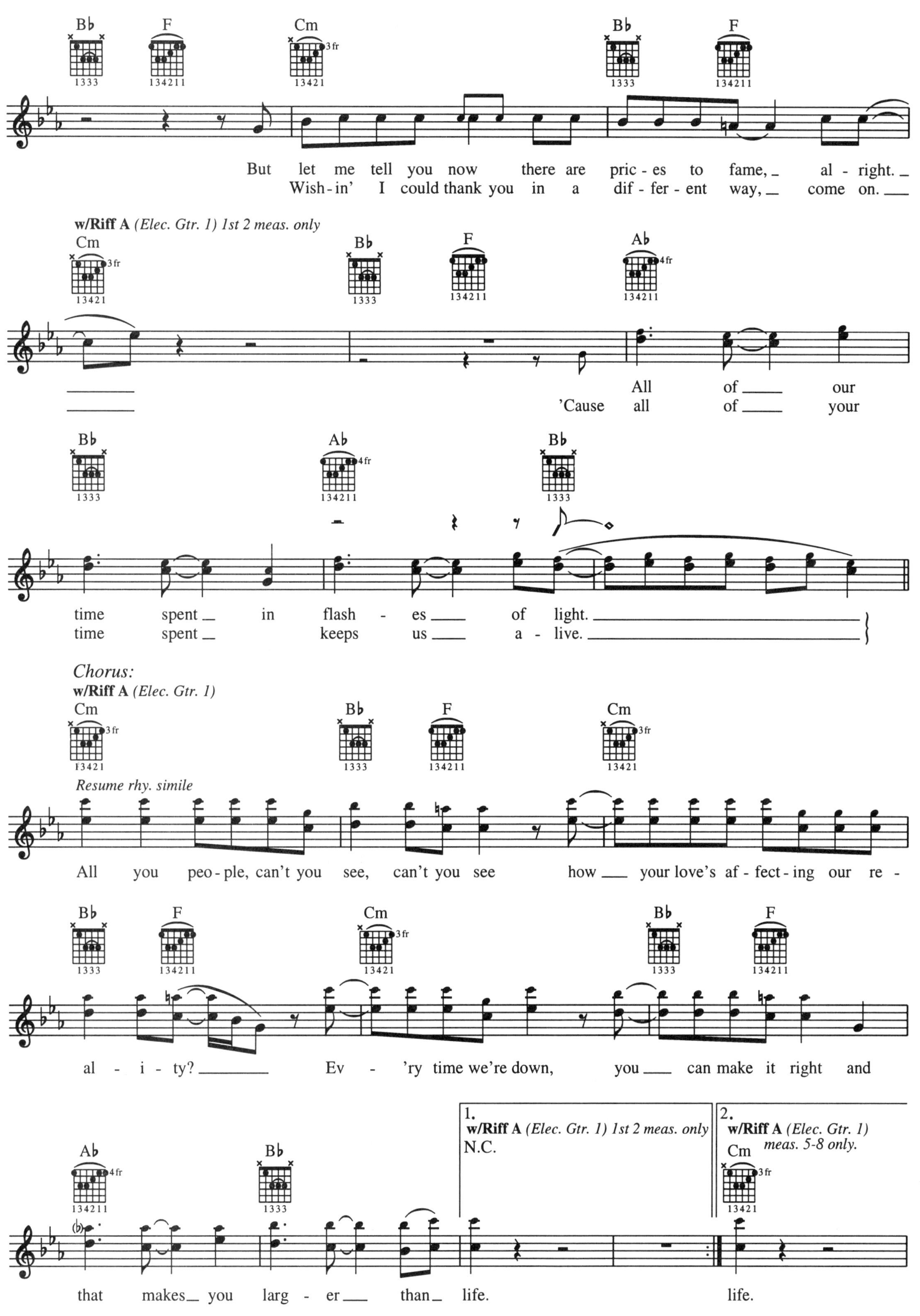
B♭ F Cm B♭ F
But let me tell you now there are pric - es to fame, al - right.
Wish - in' I could thank you in a dif - fer - ent way, come on.
w/Riff A (Elec. Gtr. 1) 1st 2 meas. only
Cm B♭ F A♭
All of our
'Cause all of your
B♭ A♭ B♭
time spent in flash - es of light.
time spent keeps us a - live.
Chorus:
w/Riff A (Elec. Gtr. 1)
Cm B♭ F Cm
Resume rhy. simile
All you peo - ple, can't you see, can't you see how your love's af - fect - ing our re -
B♭ F Cm B♭ F
al - i - ty? Ev - 'ry time we're down, you can make it right and
1.
w/Riff A (Elec. Gtr. 1) 1st 2 meas. only
N.C.
2.
w/Riff A (Elec. Gtr. 1) meas. 5-8 only.
A♭ B♭ Cm
that makes you larg - er than life.
life.

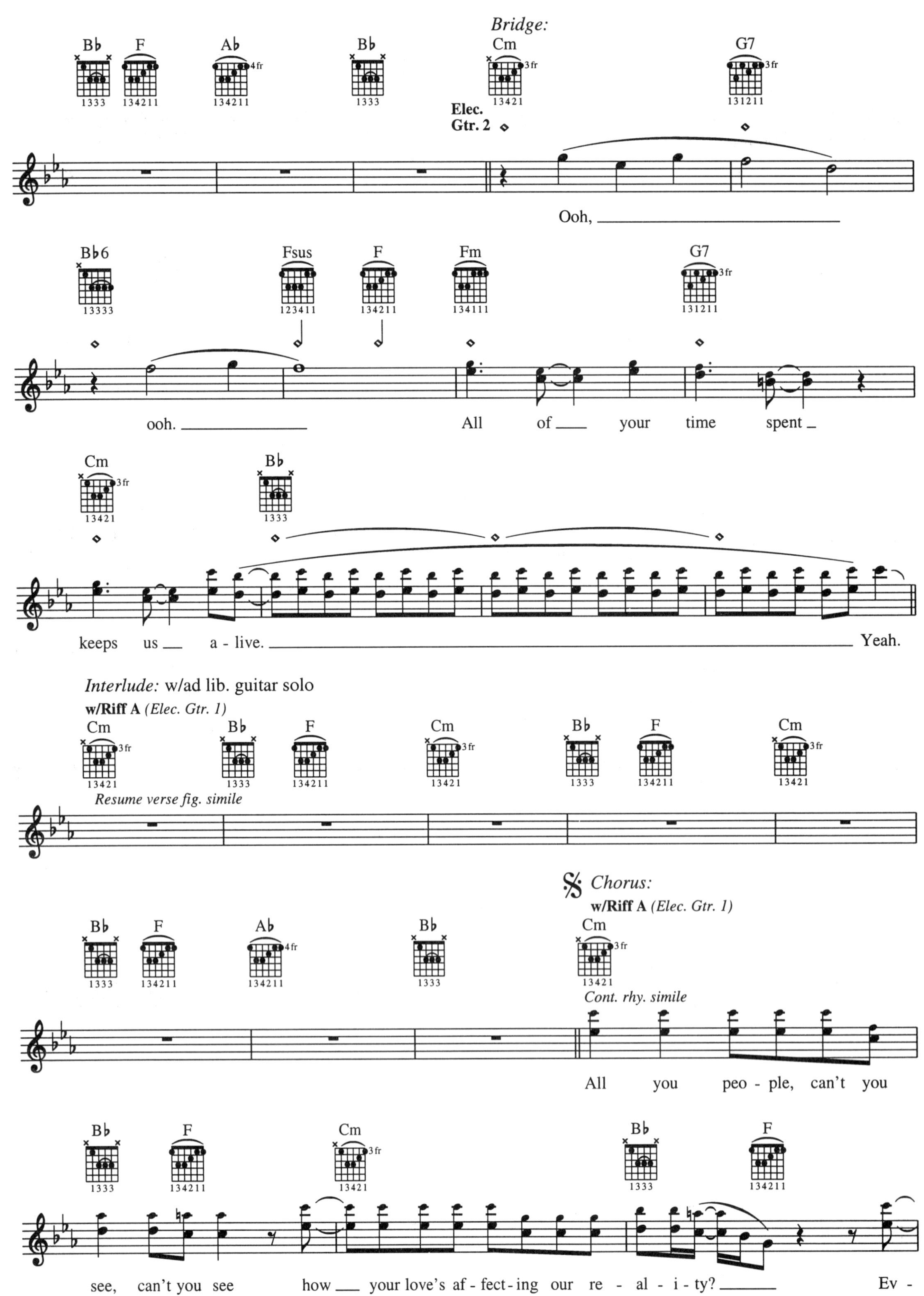

Bridge:
B♭
F
A♭
4fr
B♭
Cm
3fr
G7
3fr
Elec. Gtr. 2
Ooh,
B♭6
Fsus
F
Fm
G7
3fr
ooh.
All of your time spent
Cm
3fr
B♭
keeps us a - live.
Yeah.
Interlude: w/ad lib. guitar solo
w/Riff A (Elec. Gtr. 1)
Cm
B♭
F
Cm
B♭
F
Cm
Resume verse fig. simile
Chorus:
w/Riff A (Elec. Gtr. 1)
B♭
F
A♭
B♭
Cm
Cont. rhy. simile
All you peo - ple, can't you
B♭
F
Cm
B♭
F
see, can't you see how your love's af - fect - ing our re - al - i - ty?
Ev -

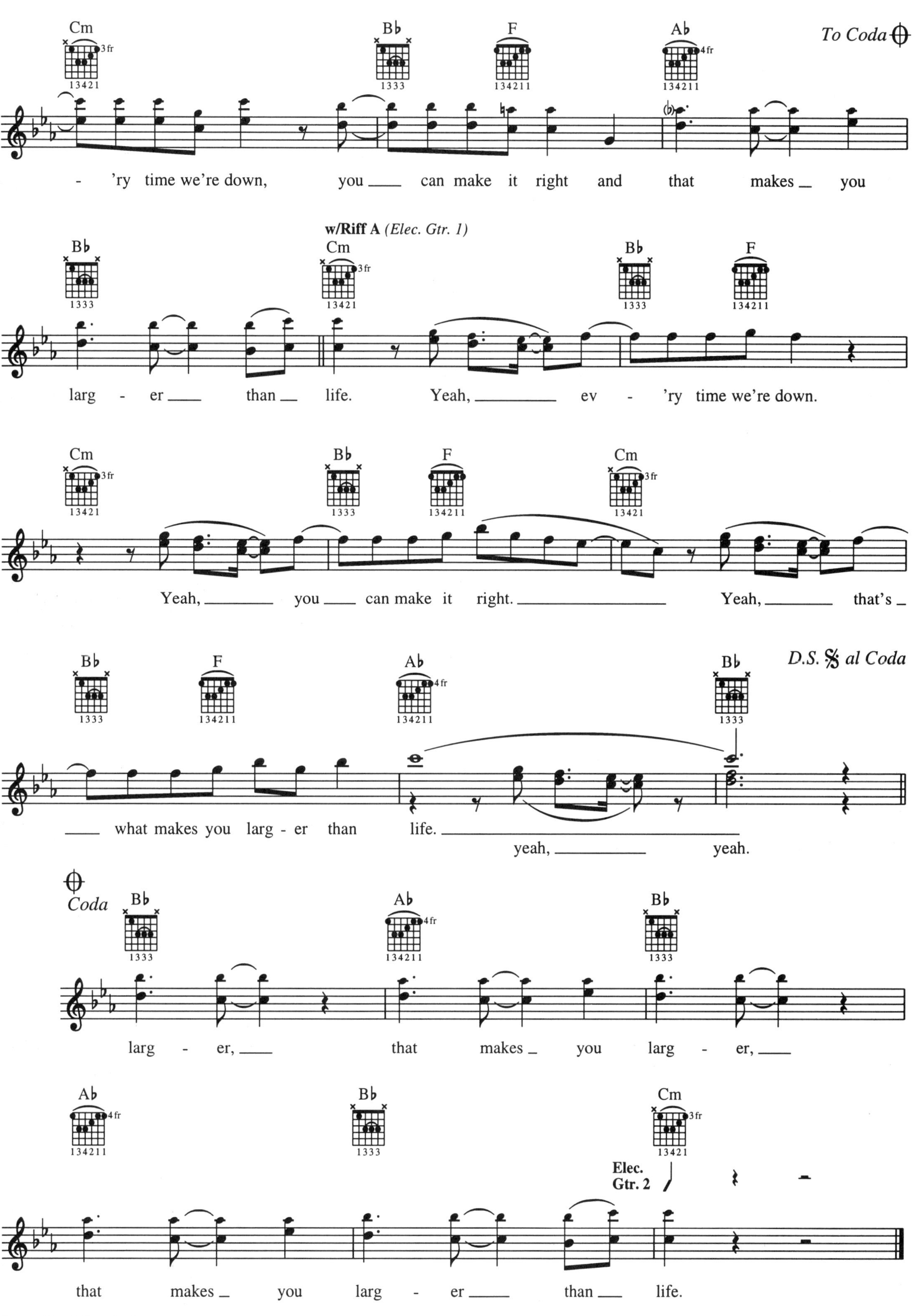
Cm
3fr
13421
Bb
1333
F
134211
Ab
4fr
134211
To Coda
- 'ry time we're down, you can make it right and that makes you
w/Riff A (Elec. Gtr. 1)
larg - er than life. Yeah, ev - 'ry time we're down.
Yeah, you can make it right. Yeah, that's
D.S. al Coda
what makes you larg - er than life.
yeah, yeah.
Coda
larg - er, that makes you larg - er,
Elec. Gtr. 2
that makes you larg - er than life.

LIVIN' LA VIDA LOCA

Words and Music by
ROBI ROSA and DESMOND CHILD

Moderately fast ♩ = 140
Intro:
C♯m
4fr
13421
Elec. Gtr. 1
Cont. rhy. simile
Horn Cue

Verse 1:
Cont. rhy. simile
She's in - to su - per - sti - tions, black cats and voo-doo dolls.

I feel a pre - mo - ni - tion, that girl's gon - na

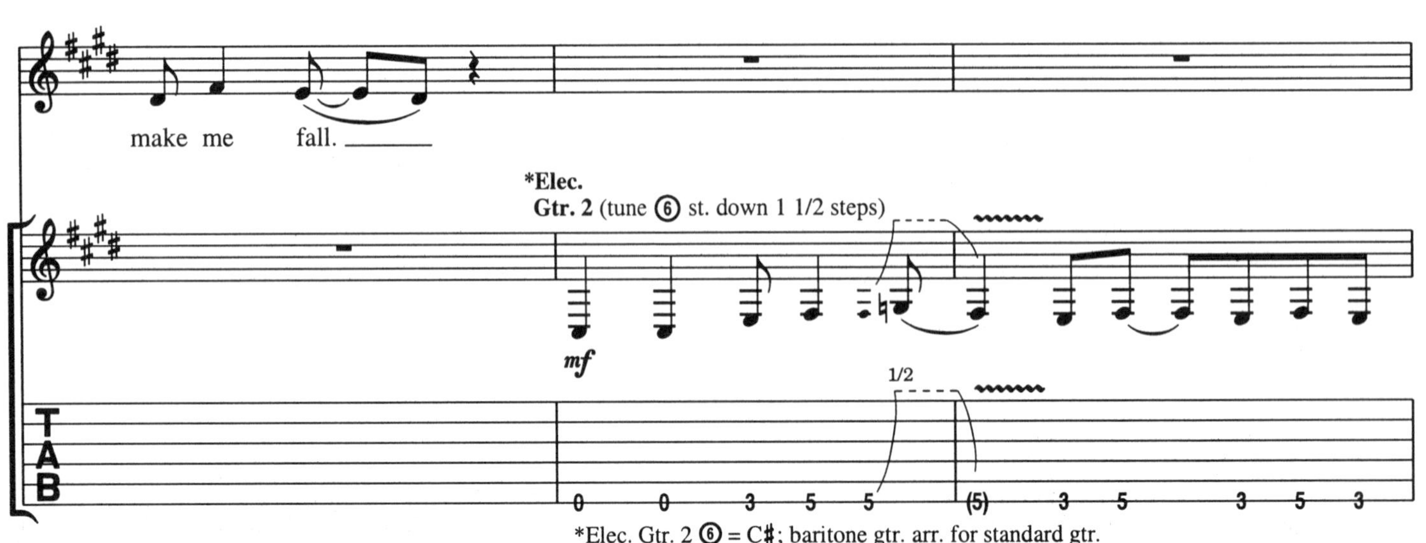
make me fall.
*Elec.
Gtr. 2 (tune ⑥ st. down 1 1/2 steps)
mf
1/2
T
A
B
0 0 3 5 5 (5) 3 5 3 5 3

*Elec. Gtr. 2 ⑥ = C♯; baritone gtr. arr. for standard gtr.

grad. slide down ⑥ st.
P.M.
T
A
B
0 0 0 3 0 0
15 15 14 14 12 12 10 10 8 8 7 7 5 5 3 3
*Mute ⑥ st. playing 1/16 notes while gradually sliding down string, pitches are approx.
Verses 2 & 3:
Cont. rhy. simile
2. She's in - to new sen - sa - tions, new kicks in the can-dle - light.
3. Woke up in New York Cit - y in a funk - y cheap ho - tel.
She's got a new ad - dic - tion for ev - 'ry day and night. She'll
She took my heart and she took my mon - ey, she must have slipped me a sleep-ing pill. She
Pre-chorus:
F♯m
134111
G♯m
4fr
134111
Cont. rhy. simile
(1.3.) make you take your clothes off and go danc - ing in the rain. She'll make
(2.) nev - er drinks the wa - ter, makes you or - der French cham-pagne.
A
111
B
1333
you live her cra - zy life, but she'll take a - way your pain, like a bul -
Once you've had a taste of her you'll nev - er be the same. Yeah, she'll make
G♯7sus
4fr
131411
Chorus:
C♯m
4fr
13421
Cont. rhy. simile
- let to your brain.
you go in - sane.
Up side, in - side out, she's

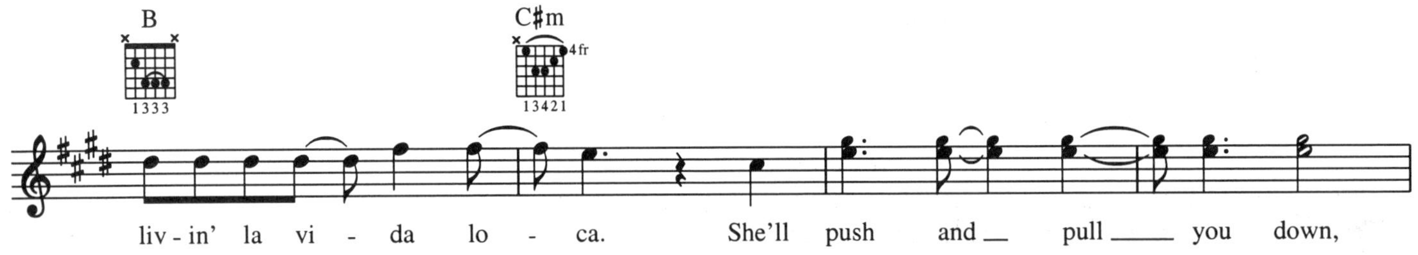
B
C♯m
liv - in' la vi - da lo - ca. She'll push and pull you down,

B
C♯m
liv - in' la vi - da lo - ca. Her lips are dev - il red and her

B
C♯m
skin's the col - or of mo - cha. She will wear you out,

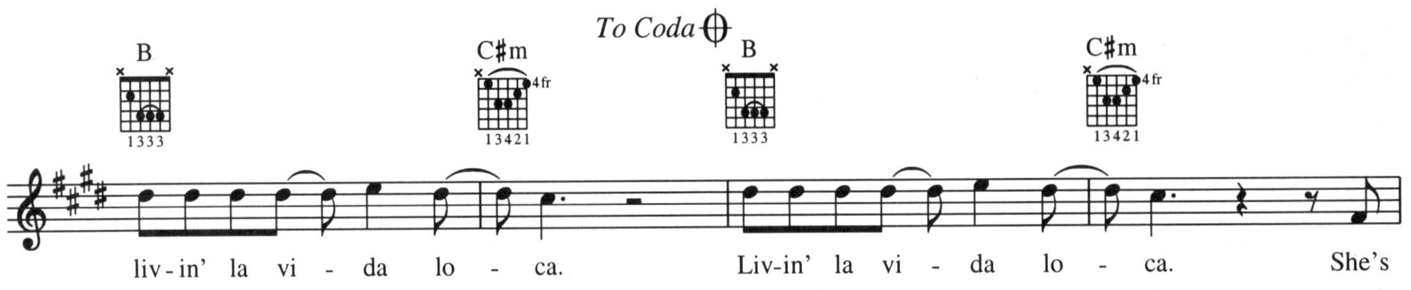
To Coda
B
C♯m
B
C♯m
liv - in' la vi - da lo - ca. Liv - in' la vi - da lo - ca. She's

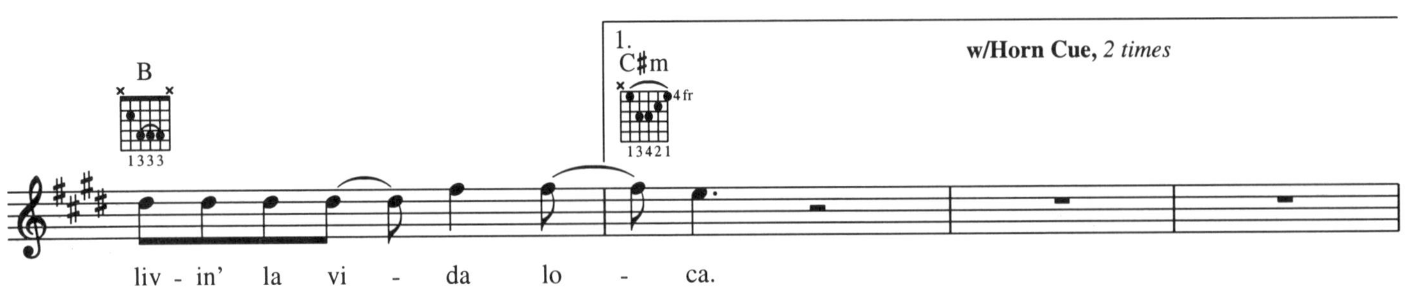
B
1.
C♯m
w/Horn Cue, 2 times
liv - in' la vi - da lo - ca.

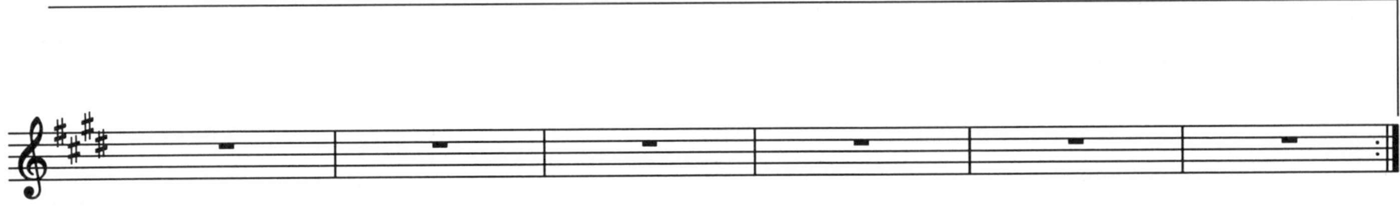

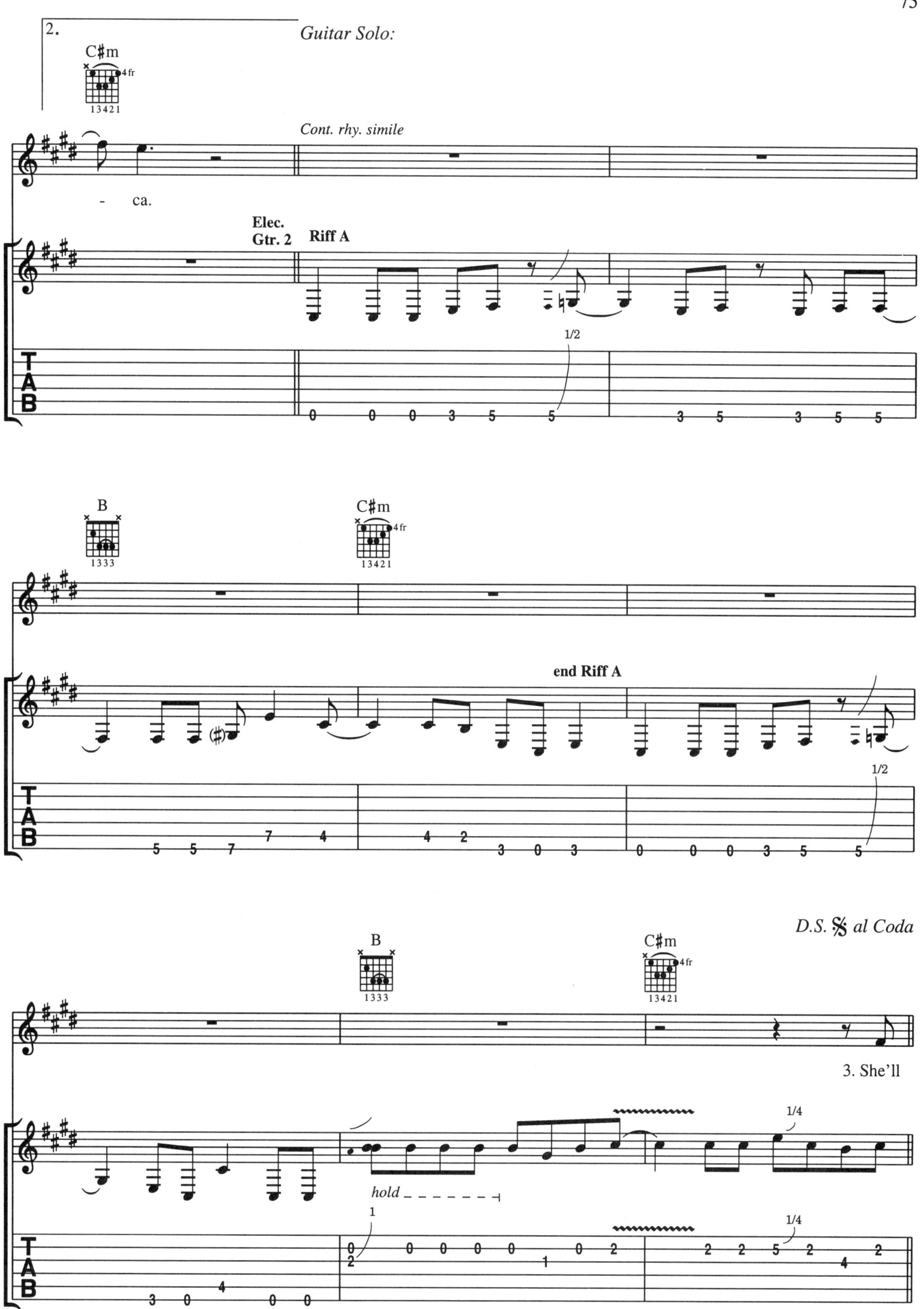
2.
Guitar Solo:
C♯m
4 fr
13421
Cont. rhy. simile
- ca.
Elec. Gtr. 2
Riff A
1/2
B
1333
C♯m
4 fr
13421
end Riff A
1/2
D.S. 𝄋 al Coda
B
1333
C♯m
4 fr
13421
3. She'll
hold
1
1/4
1/4

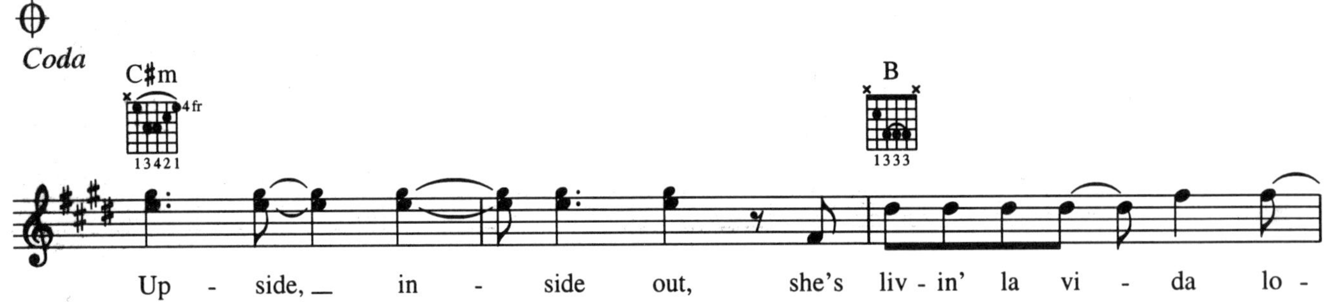
Coda
C♯m
4 fr
13421
B
1333
Up - side, in - side out, she's liv - in' la vi - da lo -

C♯m
4 fr
13421
- ca. She'll push and pull you down,

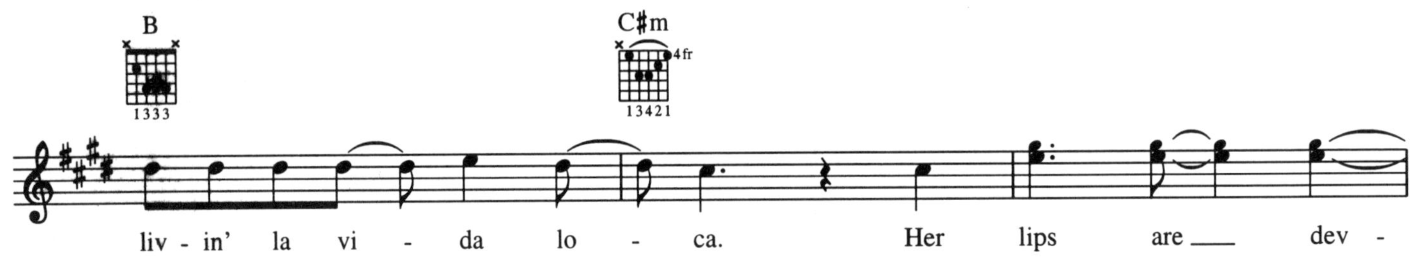
B
1333
C♯m
4 fr
13421
liv - in' la vi - da lo - ca. Her lips are dev -

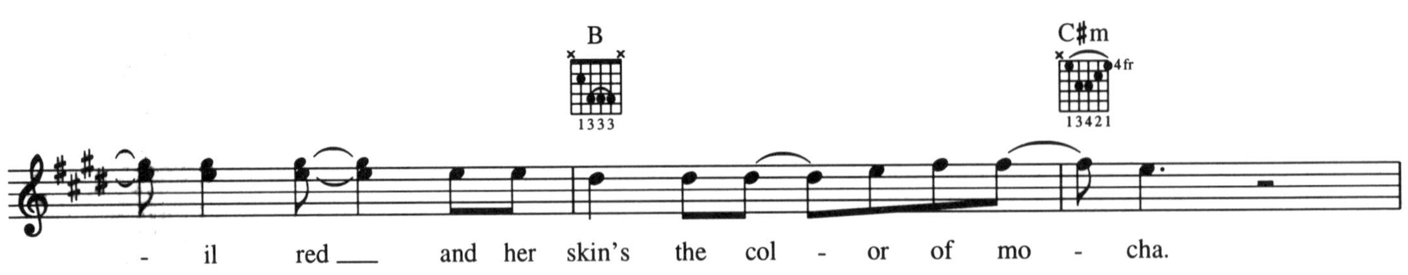
B
1333
C♯m
4 fr
13421
- il red and her skin's the col - or of mo - cha.

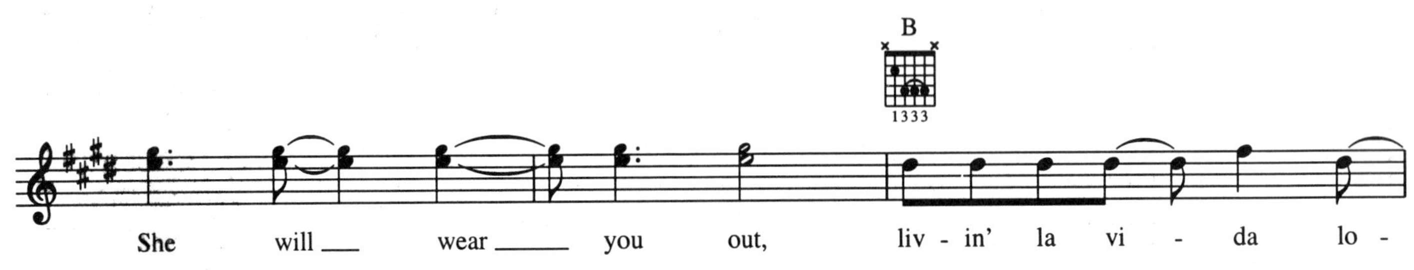
B
1333
She will wear you out, liv - in' la vi - da lo -

Outro: w/ad lib. vocal
w/Riff A *(Elec. Gtr. 2) simile*

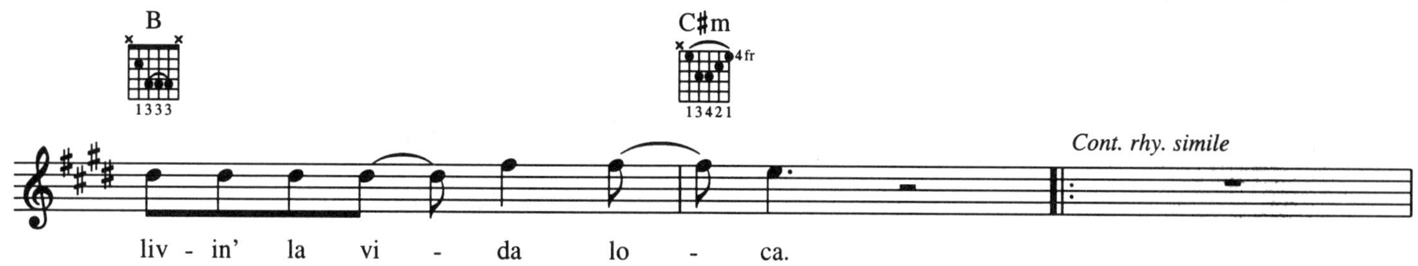

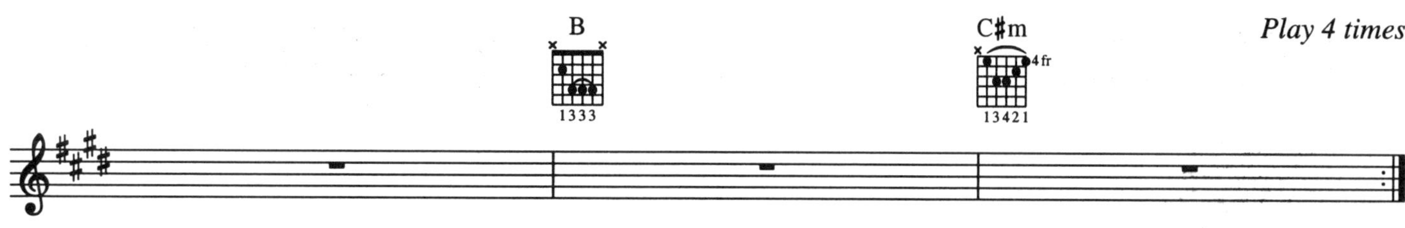

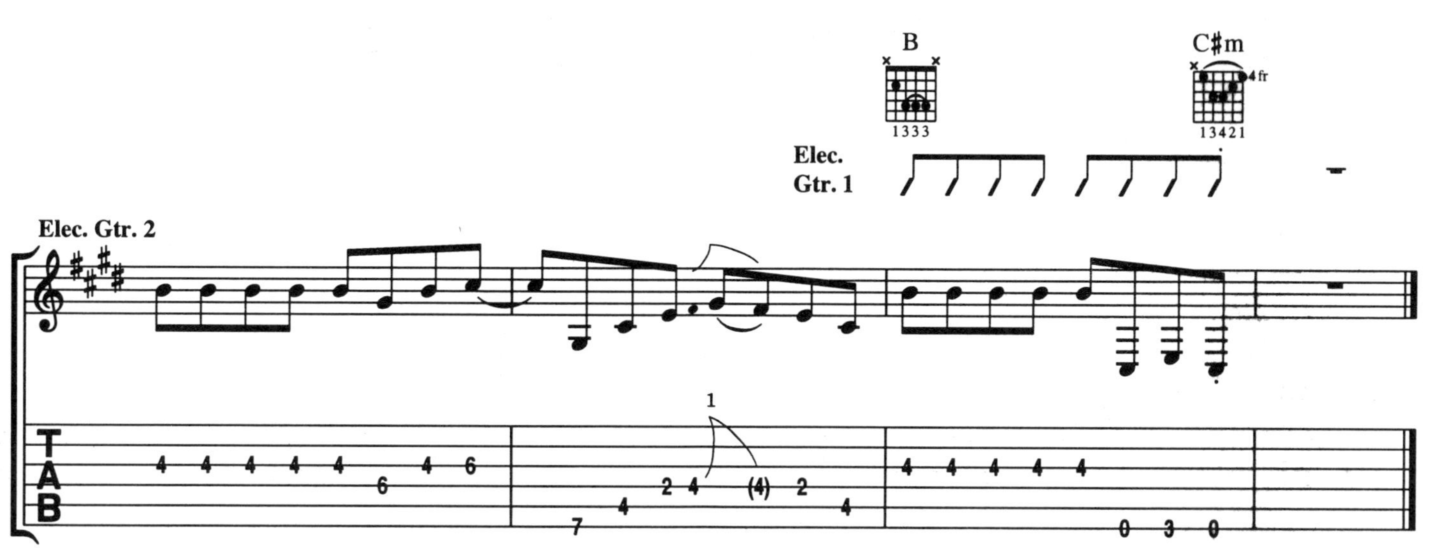

NO SCRUBS

Tune down 1/2 step:
⑥= E♭ ③= G♭
⑤= A♭ ②= B♭
④= D♭ ①= E♭

Words and Music by
KEVIN BRIGGS, KANDI BURRIS
and TAMEKA COTTLE

Moderately ♩ = 92

Intro:

Dm7 Am E7 Am

Mm, ah.

Acous. Gtr. Rhy. Fig. 1

mf hold throughout

Dm7 Am E7 Am

end Rhy. Fig. 1

Verse:

w/Rhy. Fig. 1 *(Acous. Gtr.) 2 times*

Dm7 Am E7 Am

1. Scrubs is a guy that thinks he's blind - ed, al - so known as a bust down.
2. Scrubs took to me but it's get-tin' kind-a weak and I know that he can-not ap-proach me. 'Cause I'm
(2nd time) me.

Dm7 Am E7 Am

Al - ways think-in' 'bout what he wants and just sits on his broke ass.
look-in' like that and he's look-in' like that, can't get with a pam - pered ass.
So,

Dm7 Am E7 Am
no, I don't want your num - ber. No, I don't wan - na give you mine. And
Dm7 Am E7 Am
no, I don't wan - na meet you no - where. No, or an - y old time. And

Chorus:

w/Rhy. Fig. 1 *(Acous. Gtr.) 2 times*

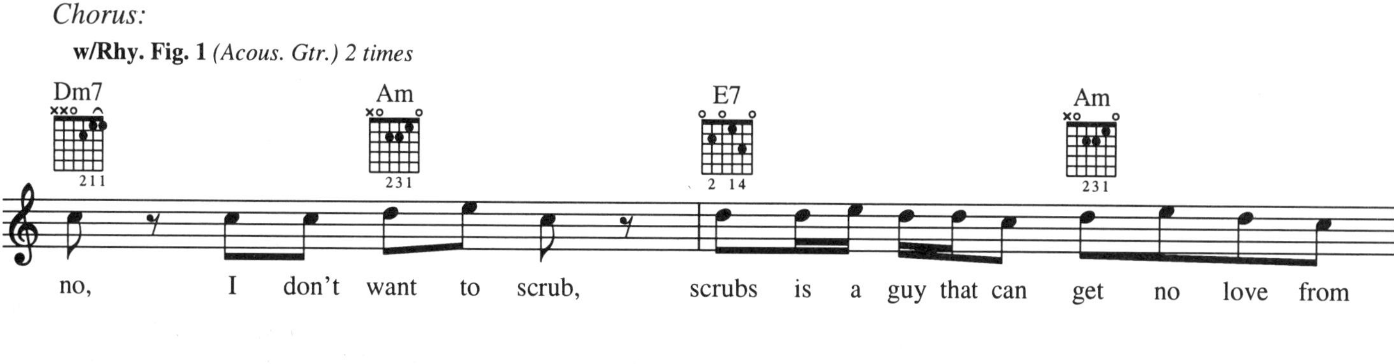
Dm7 Am E7 Am
no, I don't want to scrub, scrubs is a guy that can get no love from

Dm7 Am E7 Am Dm7 Am
me. Hang-in' out the pas-sen-ger side of his best friend's ride, try'n' to hol-ler at me. I don't want no scrub.

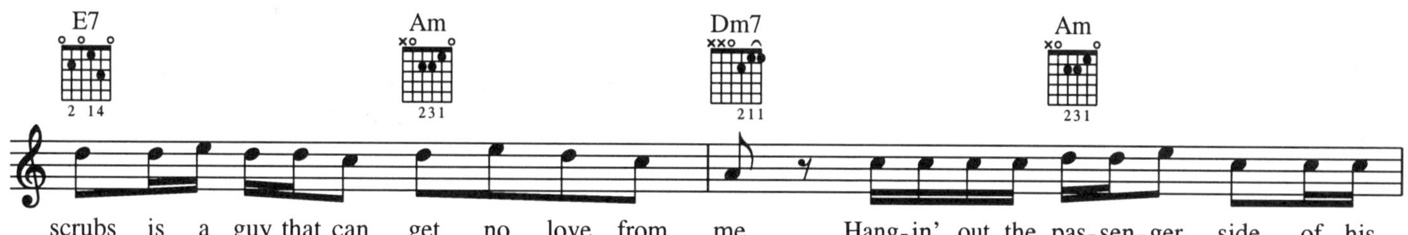
E7 Am Dm7 Am
scrubs is a guy that can get no love from me. Hang-in' out the pas-sen-ger side of his

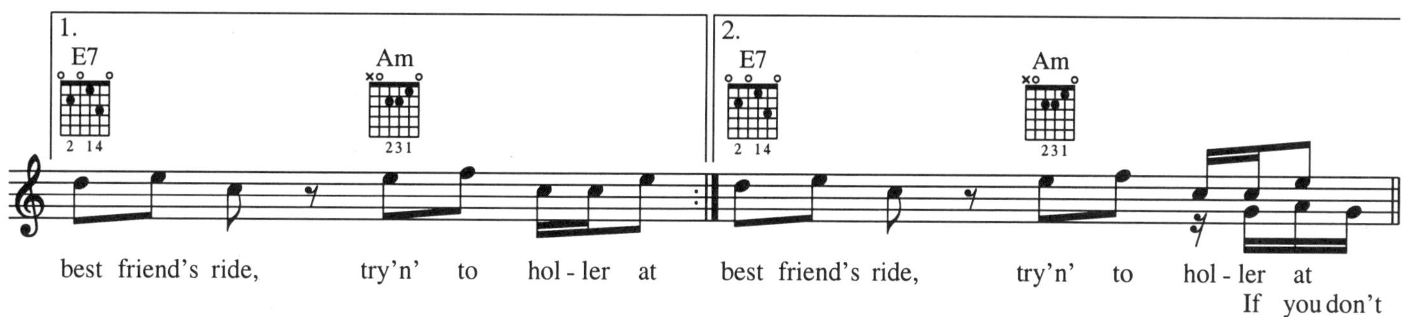
1. 2.
E7 Am E7 Am
best friend's ride, try'n' to hol - ler at best friend's ride, try'n' to hol - ler at
If you don't

Bridge:
F(9)
3214
E7(♭9)
2141
have a car and you're walk - in'.
me.
(Oh yes son, I'm talk-in' to you.)
If you
Acous. Gtr.
Am9
23
Am7
2 333
A♭7
1 243
Gm7
2 333
C7(♭9)
2131
live at home with your ma - ma.
(Oh yes son, I'm talk-in' to you.)
You
F(9)
3214
E7
1324
have it sure - ly but you don't show love.
(Oh yes, son, I'm talk-in' to you.)
Wan-na

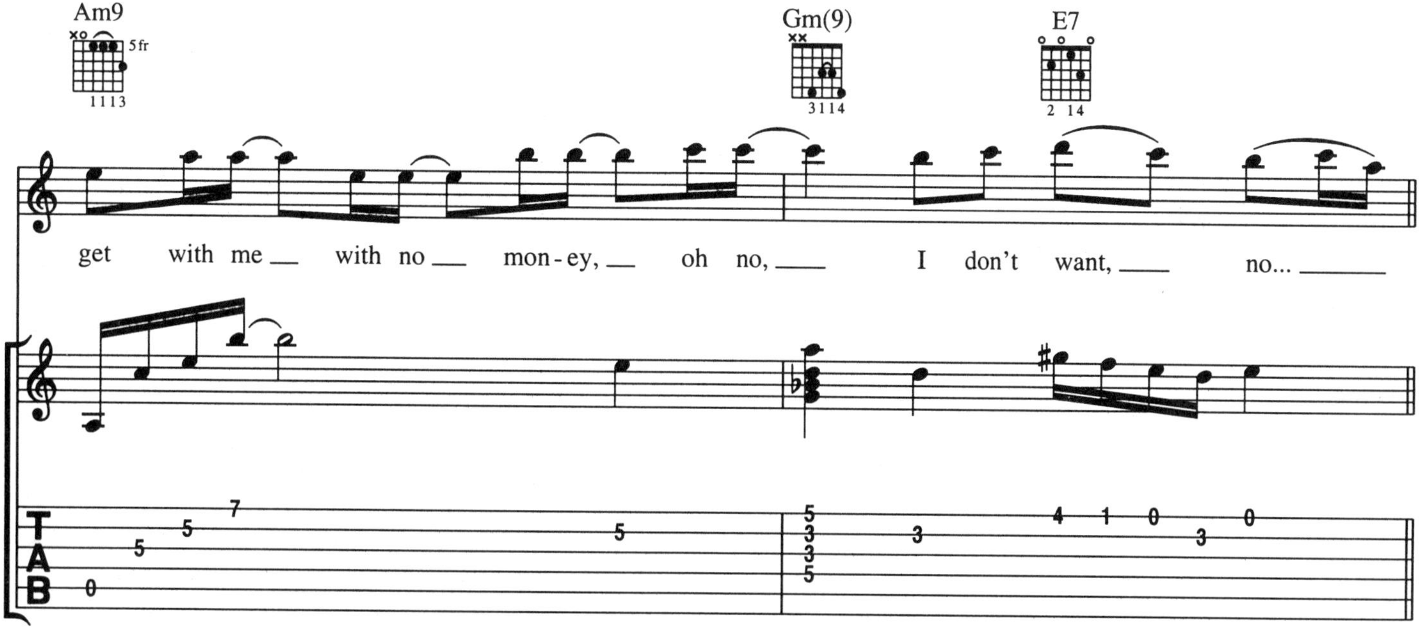
Am9
5 fr
1113
Gm(9)
3114
E7
2 14
get with me with no mon-ey, oh no, I don't want, no...
T
A
B

Interlude:

w/Rhy. Fig. 1 *(Acous. Gtr.)*

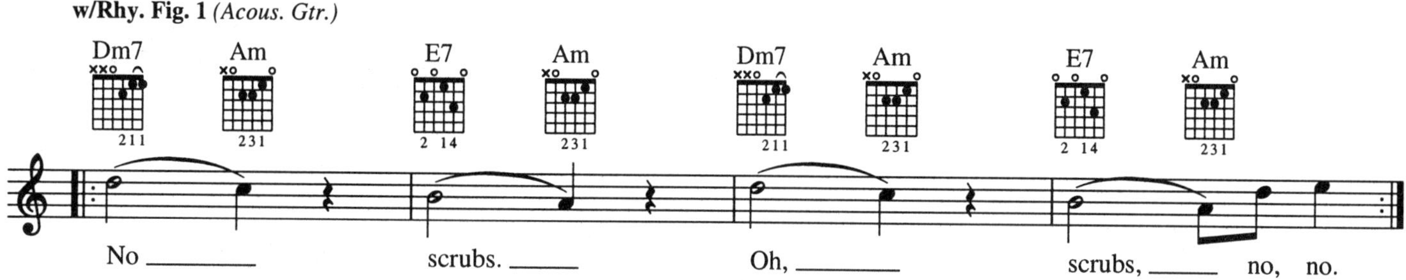
Dm7
211
Am
231
E7
2 14
Am
231
Dm7
211
Am
231
E7
2 14
Am
231
No scrubs. Oh, scrubs, no, no.

Outro:

w/Rhy. Fig. 1 *(Acous. Gtr.)*

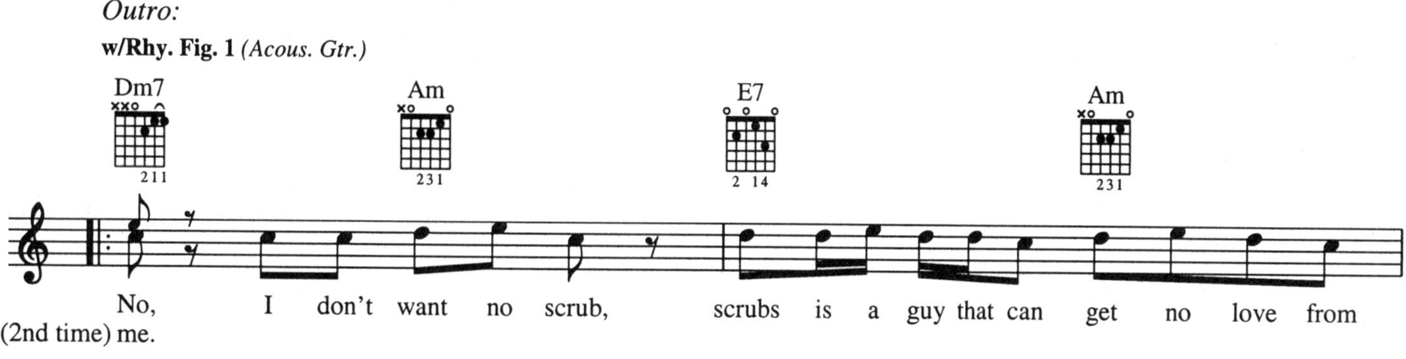
Dm7
211
Am
231
E7
2 14
Am
231
No, I don't want no scrub, scrubs is a guy that can get no love from
(2nd time) me.

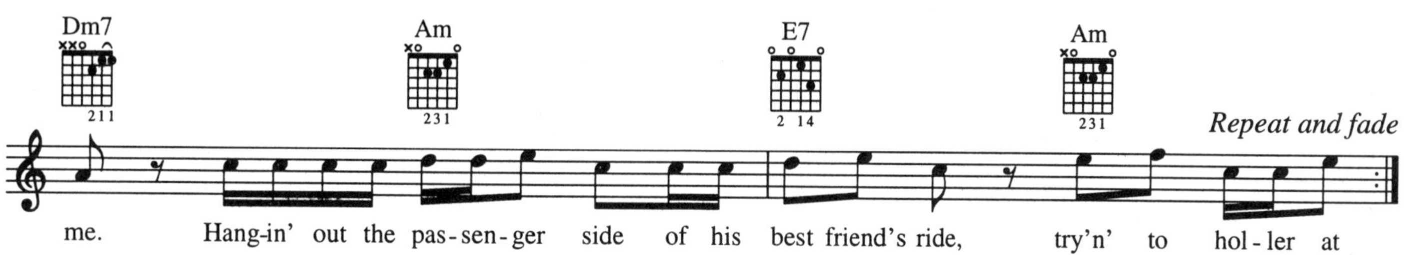
Dm7
211
Am
231
E7
2 14
Am
231
Repeat and fade
me. Hang-in' out the pas-sen-ger side of his best friend's ride, try'n' to hol-ler at

OOPS!... I DID IT AGAIN

Words and Music by
MAX MARTIN and RAMI

Oops!.. I Did It Again – 4 – 1
GFM0012

C♯m
G♯/B♯
C♯m
A
it might seem like a crush, but it does-n't mean that I'm se - ri - ous.
I cry watch-ing the days, can't you see I'm a fool in so man - y ways?
Pre-chorus:
G♯sus
G♯
F♯m7
G♯
'Cause to lose all my sens - es, that is
But to lose all my sens - es, that is
A
B5
G♯
Chorus:
C♯m
G♯
just so typ - i - c'lly me. Oh, baby, ba - by, ba - by.
just so typ - i - c'lly me. Oh, ba - by, oh.
Oops!... I did it a - gain,
C♯m
B
E
B
E
B
G♯/B♯
Cont. rhy. simile
I played with your heart, got lost in the game. Oh, ba - by, ba - by.
C♯m
G♯
C♯m
B
E
Oops!... You think I'm in love, that I'm sent from a - bove. I'm

1.
G#
C#m/G#
2.
G#
C#m
not that in-no-cent.
not that in-no-cent
Mm-hm, mm-hm.
Yeah
yeah yeah yeah yeah yeah.
Mm-hm, mm-hm.
grad. slower
Yeah yeah yeah yeah yeah yeah.
Keybd.
A tempo
Bridge:
Amaj7
B
Amaj7
(Spoken:) "Britney, before you go, there's something I want you to have." "Oh, it's beautiful! But wait a minute,
B
Amaj7
B
Bsus
G#
isn't this...?" "Yeah, it is." "But I thought the old lady dropped it into the ocean in the end." "Well, baby, I went down and got it for you."
C#m
Chorus:
G#
B5
C#m
B
Keybd.
"Oh, you shouldn't have." Oops!... I did it a-gain to your heart,

E
B
E
B
G#/B#
C#m
G#
Cont. rhy. simile
got lost in this game, oh, baby.
Oops!... You
Oops!... you
C#m
B
E
A
B
think I'm sent from above.
think that I'm sent from above.
I'm not that innocent.
Chorus:
C#m
G#
C#m
B
E/G#
B
Cont. rhy. simile
Oops!... I did it again,
I played with your heart,
got lost in the game.
E
B
G#/B#
C#m
G#
C#m
B
Oh, baby, baby. Oops!... You think I'm in love,
that I'm sent from above.
1.
E
G#
B5
I'm not the innocent.
2.
E
G#
N.C.
I'm not that innocent.

SHE'S ALL I EVER HAD

Words and Music by
ROBI ROSA, GEORGE NORIEGA
and JON SECADA

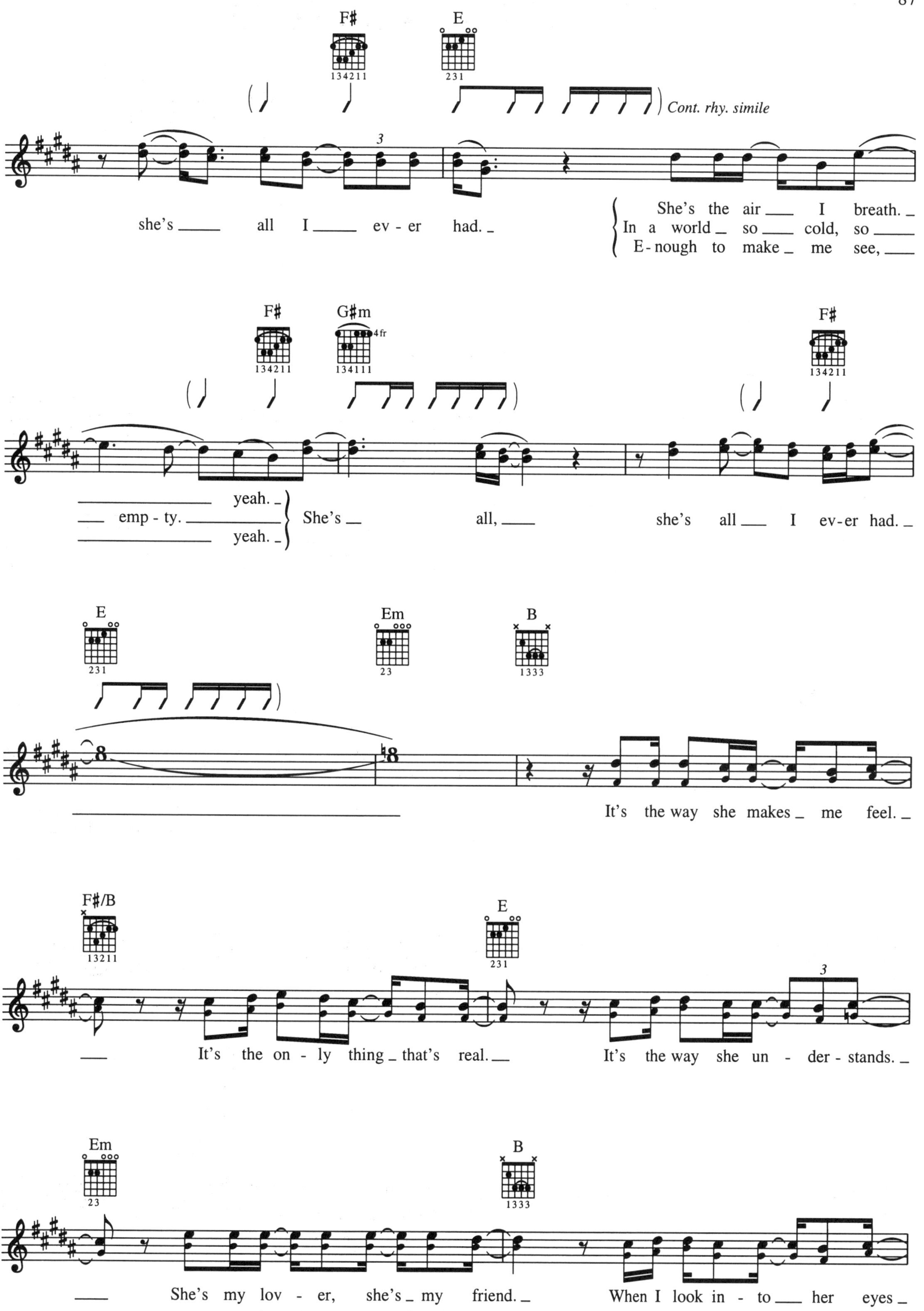
F♯
E
Cont. rhy. simile
she's all I ever had.
She's the air I breath.
In a world so cold, so
E-nough to make me see,
F♯
G♯m
F♯
yeah.
empty.
yeah.
She's all,
she's all I ev-er had.
E
Em
B
It's the way she makes me feel.
F♯/B
E
It's the on-ly thing that's real.
It's the way she un-der-stands.
Em
B
She's my lov-er, she's my friend.
When I look in-to her eyes

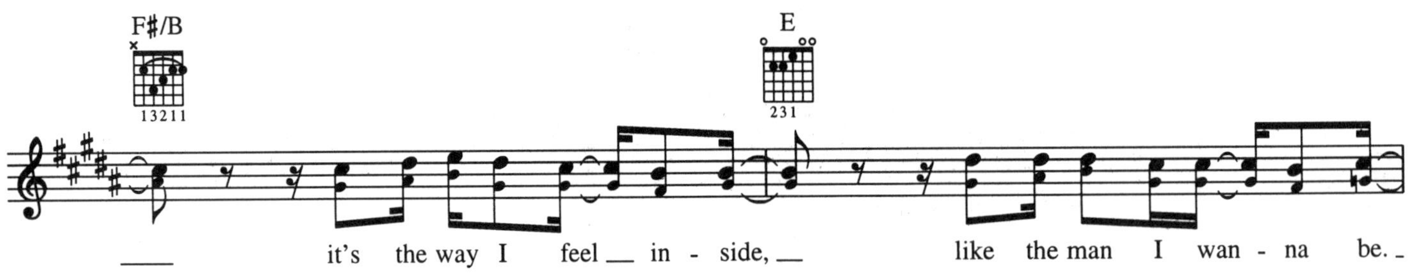
F#/B
13211
E
231
it's the way I feel in - side,
like the man I wan - na be.

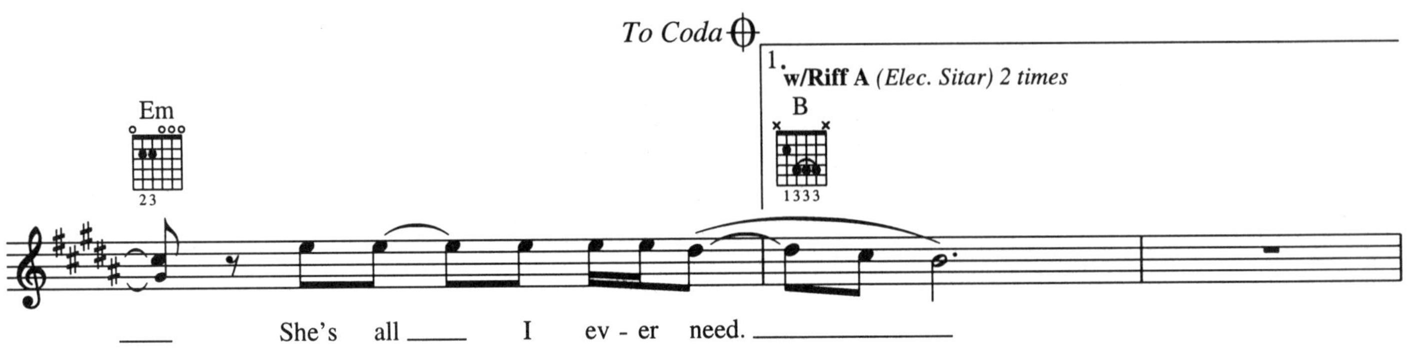
To Coda
1.
w/Riff A (Elec. Sitar) 2 times
Em
23
B
1333
She's all I ev - er need.

2.
w/Riff A (Elec. Sitar) 2 times
B
1333

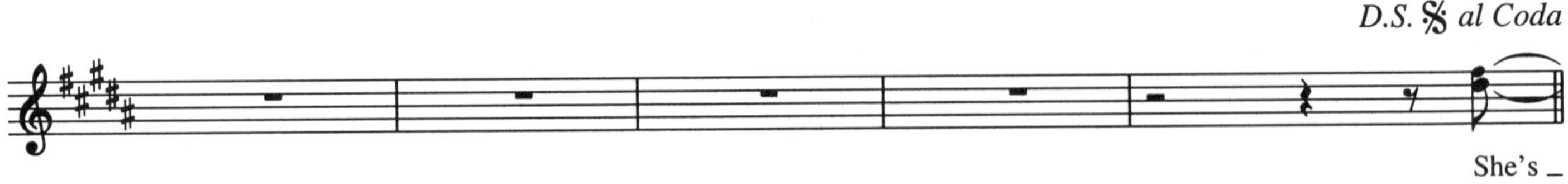
D.S. al Coda
She's

Coda
B
1333
F#/B
13211
It's the way she makes me feel.
It's the on - ly thing that's real.

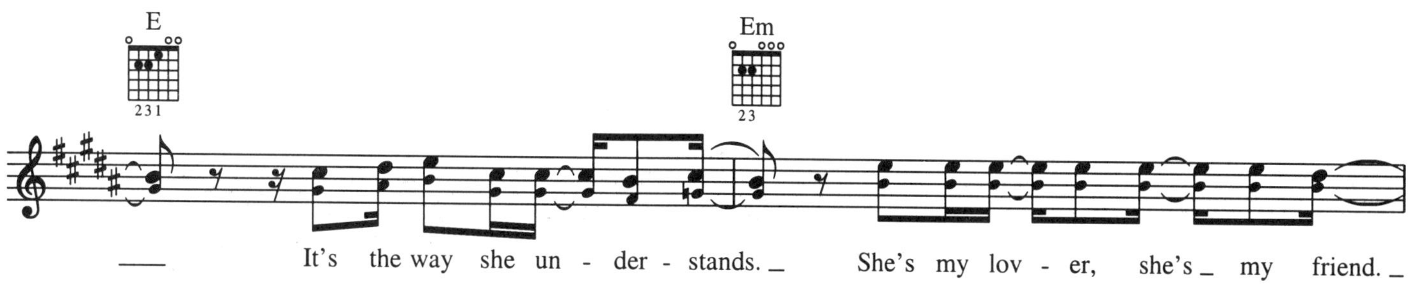
E
231
Em
23
It's the way she un - der - stands. She's my lov - er, she's my friend.

B
1333
F♯/B
13211
When I look in - to her eyes, it's the way I feel in - side,

E
231
Em
23
like the man I wan - na be. She's all I ev - er need.

Outro:

w/Riff A (Elec. Sitar) 2 times, simile
B
1333

B
1333
Acous. Gtr.
Here I am.

SHOW ME THE MEANING OF BEING LONELY

Words and Music by
MAX MARTIN and HERBERT CRICHLOW

F#m
D
E
F#m
nights of light so soon be - come
guilt - y roads to an end - less love,
wild and free, I could
there's no con - trol. Are you
D
E
D
C#7sus
C#7
feel the sun. Your ev - 'ry wish will be done, they tell me...
with me now? Your ev - 'ry wish will be done, they tell me...
Chorus:
F#m
D
E
F#m
Cont. rhy. simile
Show me the mean-ing of be - ing lone - ly. Is this the feel-ing I
D
E
A
C#7
need to walk with? Tell me why I can't be there where you are.
F#m
1. w/Riff A (Nylon-str. Gtr.)
D
E
F#m
D
E
There's some-thing miss-ing in my heart.
2.
Bridge:
D
E
G#m
E
F#
Acous. Gtr.
Acous. Gtr.
some-thing miss-ing in my heart. There's no-where to run, I have no place to go.

G♯m
E
F♯
B
134111
231
134211
1333
Sur - ren - der my heart, body - y and soul. How can it be you're ask - ing me
D♯7sus
D♯7
1324
to feel the things you nev - er show?
Resume verse fig. simile
Nylon-str. Gtr.
You are miss - ing in my heart.

D♯7
G♯m
E
F♯
Tell me why I can't be there where you are.
Chorus:
G♯m
E
F♯
G♯m
Cont. rhy. simile
Show me the feel-ing of be-ing lone-ly. Is this the feel-ing I
(first time only)
E
F♯
B
D♯7
G♯m
need to walk with? Tell me why I can't be there where you are. There's
1.
E
F♯
2.
E
F♯
G♯m
Acous. Gtr.
some-thing miss-ing in my heart. some-thing miss-ing in my heart.

UNPRETTY (DON'T LOOK ANY FURTHER)

Words and Music by FRANNE GOLDE, DENNIS LAMBERT, DUANE HITCHINGS, DALLAS AUSTIN and TIONNE WATKINS

C
G/B
C
F/A
G/B
Same old me a - gain to - day, yeah.
May - be get rid of you and then I'll get back to me.
I have
size, look cool, eye size - a - ble.
Ev - 'ry-time I think I'm through it's be -
cause of you.
I tried dif - f'rent ways but it's all the same.
At the
end of the day I have my - self to blame, I'm just trip - pin'.
Chorus:
w/Rhy. Fig. 1 (Acous. Gtr.) 4 times
You can buy your hair if it won't grow.
You can fix your nose if he says so.
You can buy all the make-up the man can make.
But if you can't look in - side you,
find out who am I too.
Be in the po - si - tion to make me

1.
w/Rhy. Fig. 1 (Acous. Gtr.) 2 times
F/A G/B C G/B C F/A G/B
feel so damn un - pret-ty. Yeah, and make you feel un - pret-ty too.
C G/B C F/A G/B
2.
w/Rhy. Fig. 1 (Acous. Gtr.) 4 times
C G/B C
You can buy your hair if it won't grow.
F/A G/B C G/B C
You can fix your nose if he says so. You can buy all the make - up the
F/A G/B C G/B C F/A G/B
man can make. But if you can't look in - side you, find out who am I too.
C G/B C F/A G/B
Be in the po - si - tion to make me feel so damn un - pret - ty.
Interlude:
w/Rhy. Fig. 1 (Acous. Gtr.) 4 times
w/Rhy. Fig. 1A (Elec. Gtr.) 4 times, simile
C G/B C F/A G/B C G/B C
And make you feel un - pret-ty too.

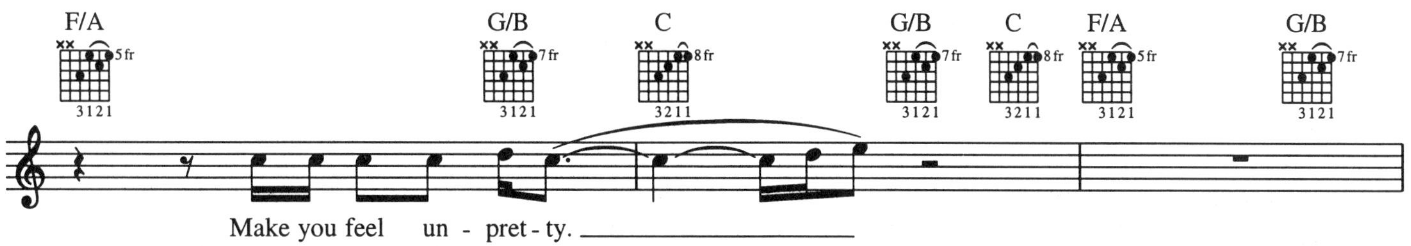
F/A G/B C G/B C F/A G/B
Make you feel un - pret - ty.

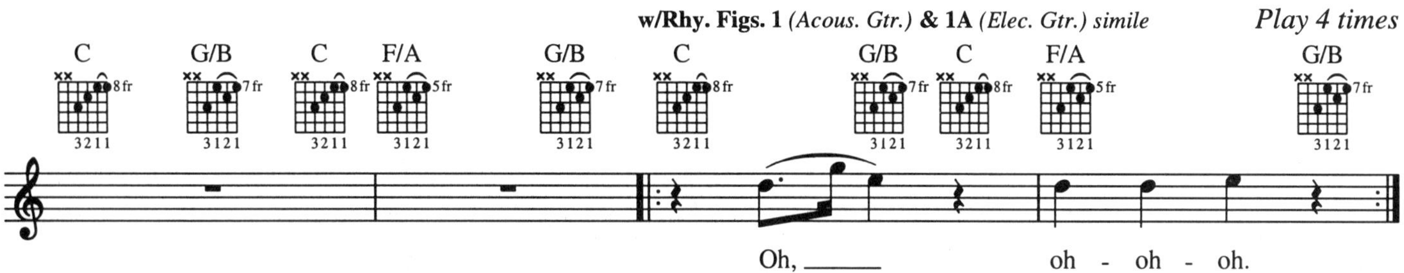
w/Rhy. Figs. 1 (Acous. Gtr.) & 1A (Elec. Gtr.) simile
Play 4 times
C G/B C F/A G/B C G/B C F/A G/B
Oh, oh - oh - oh.

Chorus:

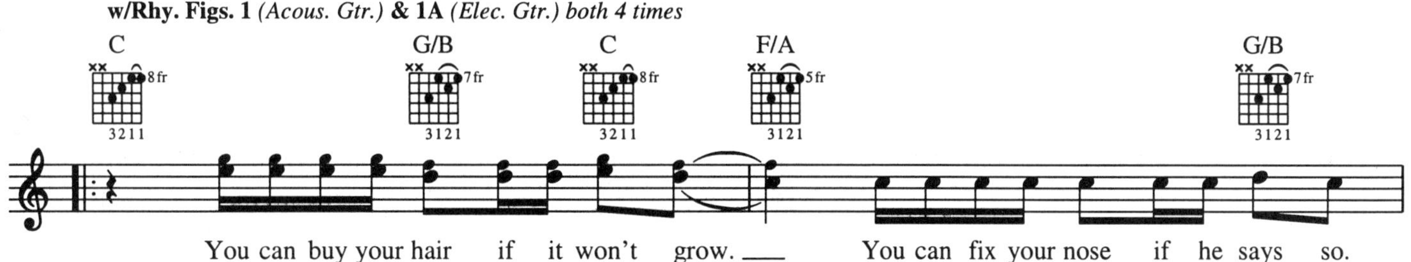
w/Rhy. Figs. 1 (Acous. Gtr.) & 1A (Elec. Gtr.) both 4 times
C G/B C F/A G/B
You can buy your hair if it won't grow. You can fix your nose if he says so.

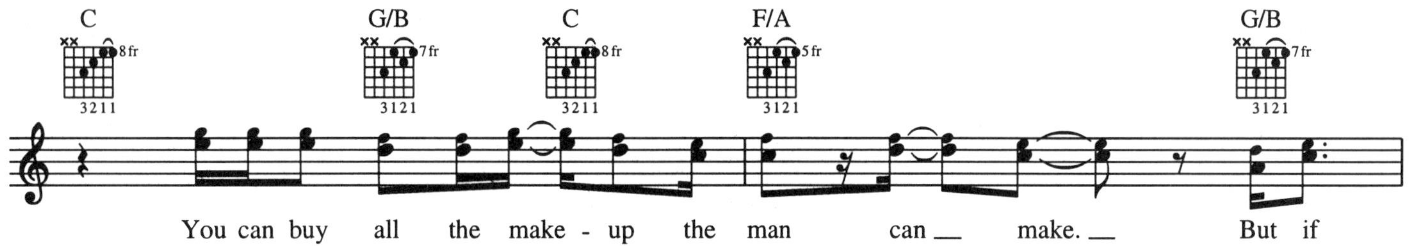
C G/B C F/A G/B
You can buy all the make - up the man can make. But if

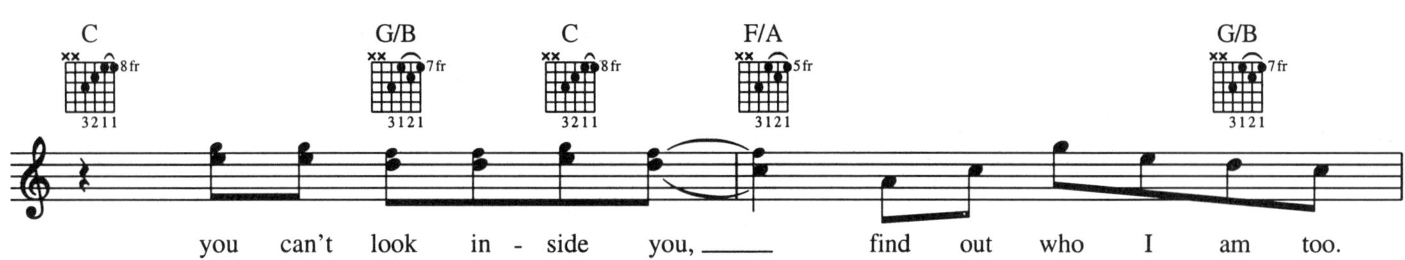
C G/B C F/A G/B
you can't look in - side you, find out who I am too.

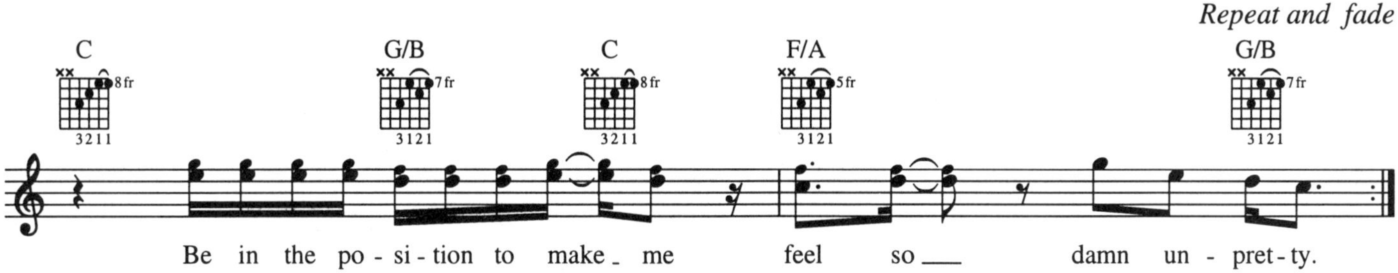
Repeat and fade
C G/B C F/A G/B
Be in the po - si - tion to make me feel so damn un - pret - ty.

WHAT A GIRL WANTS

Words and Music by GUY ROCHE
and SHELLY PEIKEN

Verse:
F♯m
3111
C♯m7
4 fr
13121
1. I wan - na thank you for giv - ing me time to breathe.
man might have walked a - way, but you had faith.
end Rhy. Fig. 1
Like a rock, you wait - ed so pa - tient - ly while I get it to - geth -
Strong e - nough to move o - ver and give me space while I get it to - geth -
er, hmmm, while I fig - ured it out.
er, yeah, while I fig - ured it out. They

F♯m
C♯m7
F♯m
I on - ly looked, but I nev - er touched 'cause in my heart was a
say if you love some-thing let it go, if it comes back it's yours.
C♯m7
Bm7
pic - ture of us hold - in' hands, mak - in' plans, and it's
That's how you know it's for keeps, yeah, it's for sure, and you're
D6/E
luck - y for me you un - der - stand.
read - y and will - ing to give me more than...
What a girl
Cont. in slashes

Chorus:
A
Amaj7/E*
A9
Acous. Gtr.
Cont. rhy. simile
wants, what a girl needs, what-ev-er makes me hap-py sets
*Bass plays E.
Dmaj7
Dm7
G9
you free, and I'm thank-ing you for know-ing ex-act-ly. for giv-ing it to me.
What a girl wants, what a girl needs, what-ev-er keeps me in
To Coda
1.
w/Rhy. Fig. 1
(Acous. Gtr.)
F♯m
your arms and I'm thank-ing you for be-ing there for me.
2.
2. A weak-er
Oh, ba-by.
Oh, dar-ling, thank you, thank you. A

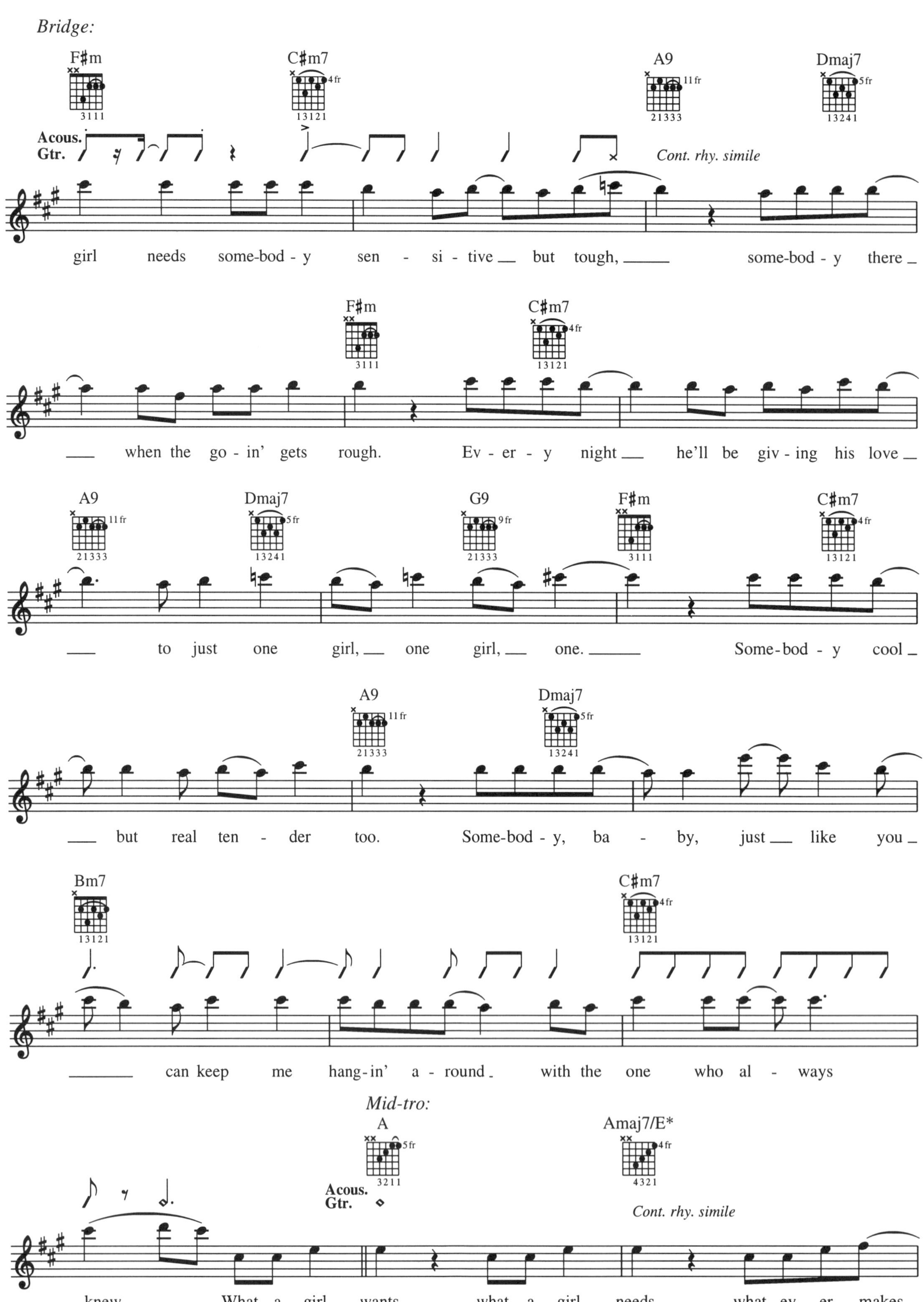
Bridge:
F♯m
C♯m7
A9
Dmaj7
Acous. Gtr.
Cont. rhy. simile
girl needs some-bod - y sen - si - tive but tough, some-bod - y there
when the go - in' gets rough. Ev - er - y night he'll be giv - ing his love
G9
to just one girl, one girl, one. Some-bod - y cool
but real ten - der too. Some-bod - y, ba - by, just like you
Bm7
can keep me hang-in' a - round with the one who al - ways
Mid-tro:
A
Amaj7/E*
knew... What a girl wants, what a girl needs, what-ev - er makes

A9
Dmaj7
Dm7
G9
me hap - py sets you free.
A
Amaj7/E*
A9
What a girl wants, what a girl needs, what - ev - er keeps me in
Dmaj7
Dm7
G9
D.S. al Coda
your arms.
What a girl
Coda
G9
F♯m
C♯m7
be - ing there. What a girl wants, what a girl needs, what - ev - er makes
A9
Dmaj7
Dm7
G9
me hap - py sets you free and I'm thank - ing you for know-ing ex - act - ly.
Outro: w/ad lib. vocal
F♯m
A9
Dmaj7
G9
Repeat and fade
Acous. Gtr.

(YOU DRIVE ME) CRAZY

Words and Music by JORGEN ELOFSSON,
DAVID KREUGER, PER MAGNUSSON and
MAX MARTIN

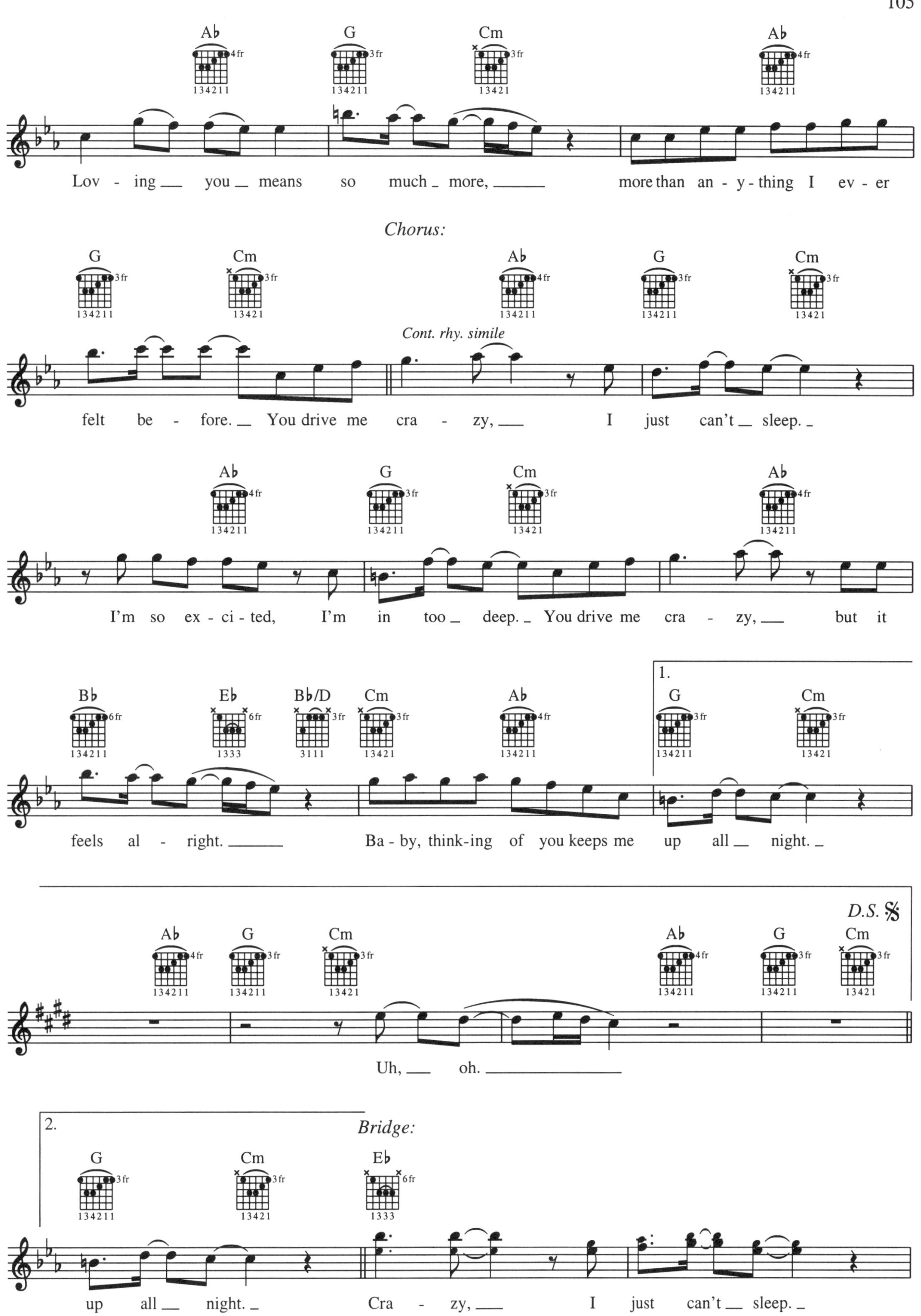
Ab
G
Cm
Ab
Lov - ing you means so much more, more than an - y - thing I ev - er
Chorus:
G
Cm
Ab
G
Cm
Cont. rhy. simile
felt be - fore. You drive me cra - zy, I just can't sleep.
Ab
G
Cm
Ab
I'm so ex - ci - ted, I'm in too deep. You drive me cra - zy, but it
1.
Bb
Eb
Bb/D
Cm
Ab
G
Cm
feels al - right. Ba - by, think-ing of you keeps me up all night.
D.S.
Ab
G
Cm
Ab
G
Cm
Uh, oh.
2.
Bridge:
G
Cm
Eb
up all night. Cra - zy, I just can't sleep.

C♭maj7
I'm so ex - cit - ed, I'm in too deep. Cra - zy but it
B♭m7
E♭m7
C♭
B♭7sus
B♭7
Cm
A♭
G
Cm
feels al - right. Ev-'ry day and ev - 'ry night.
w/ad lib. guitar solo
Chorus:
You drive me cra - zy,
(You drive me cra - zy, ba - by.)
I'm so ex - cit - ed, I'm in too deep. Oh, cra - zy but it
B♭
E♭
B♭/D
feels al - right. Ba - by, think-ing of you keeps me up all night. You drive me
1.
2.
Fm
Elec. Gtr.
up all night. Ba - by, think-ing of you keeps me up all night.

GUITAR TAB GLOSSARY **

TABLATURE EXPLANATION

READING TABLATURE: Tablature illustrates the six strings of the guitar. Notes and chords are indicated by the placement of fret numbers on a given string(s).

BENDING NOTES

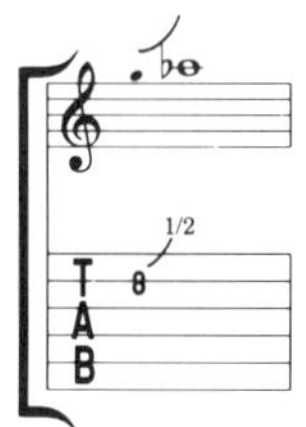

HALF STEP: Play the note and bend string one half step.*

WHOLE STEP: Play the note and bend string one whole step.

WHOLE STEP AND A HALF: Play the note and bend string a whole step and a half.

SLIGHT BEND (Microtone): Play the note and bend string slightly to the equivalent of half a fret.

*A half step is the smallest interval in Western music; it is equal to one fret. A whole step equals two frets.

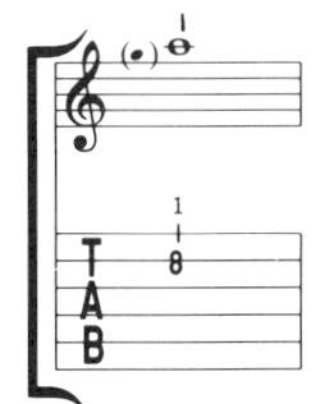

PREBEND (Ghost Bend): Bend to the specified note, before the string is picked.

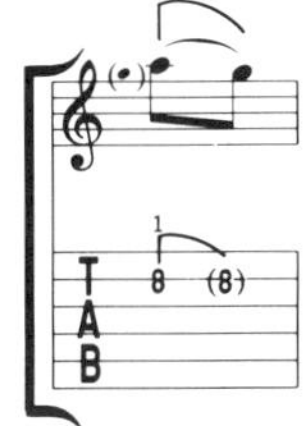

PREBEND AND RELEASE: Bend the string, play it, then release to the original note.

REVERSE BEND: Play the already-bent string, then immediately drop it down to the fretted note.

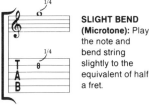

BEND AND RELEASE: Play the note and gradually bend to the next pitch, then release to the original note. Only the first note is attacked.

UNISON BEND: Play both notes and immediately bend the lower note to the same pitch as the higher note.

DOUBLE NOTE BEND: Play both notes and immediately bend both strings simultaneously.

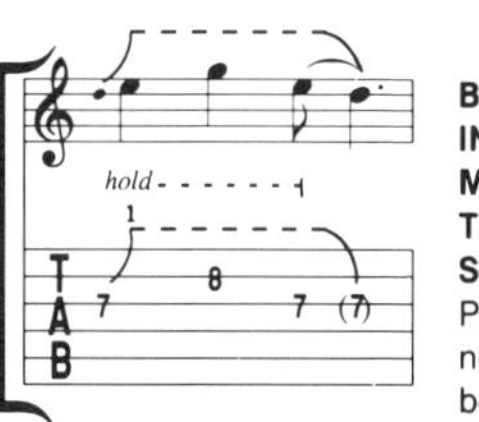

BENDS INVOLVING MORE THAN ONE STRING: Play the note and bend string while playing an additional note (or notes) on another string(s). Upon release, relieve pressure from additional note(s), causing original note to sound alone.

BENDS INVOLVING STATIONARY NOTES: Play notes and bend lower pitch, then hold until release begins (indicated at the point where line becomes solid).

TREMOLO BAR

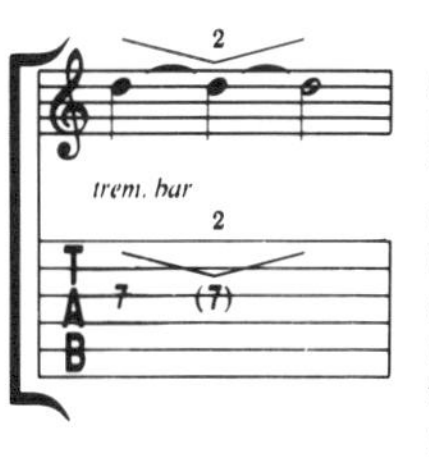

SPECIFIED INTERVAL: The pitch of a note or chord is lowered to a specified interval and then may or may not return to the original pitch. The activity of the tremolo bar is graphically represented by peaks and valleys.

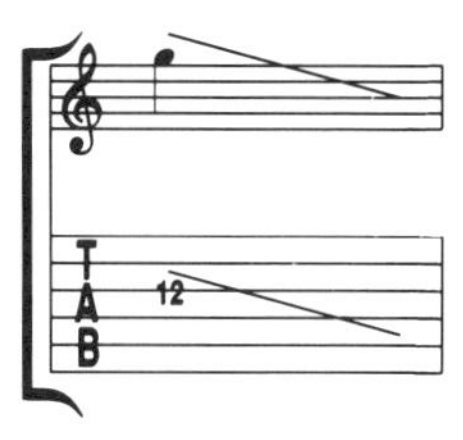

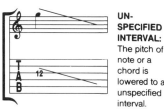

UN-SPECIFIED INTERVAL: The pitch of a note or a chord is lowered to an unspecified interval.

HARMONICS

NATURAL HARMONIC: A finger of the fret hand lightly touches the note or notes indicated in the tab and is played by the pick hand.

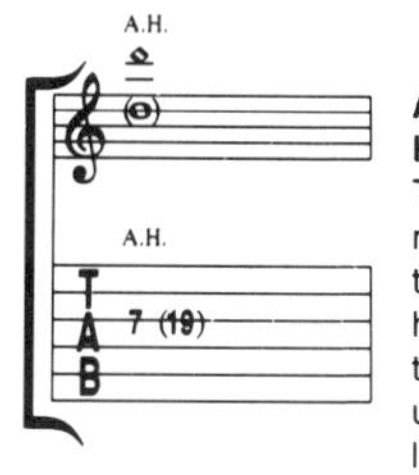

ARTIFICIAL HARMONIC: The first tab number is fretted, then the pick hand produces the harmonic by using a finger to lightly touch the same string at the second tab number (in parenthesis) and is then picked by another finger.

ARTIFICIAL "PINCH" HARMONIC: A note is fretted as indicated by the tab, then the pick hand produces the harmonic by squeezing the pick firmly while using the tip of the index finger in the pick attack. If parenthesis are found around the fretted note, it does not sound. No parenthesis means both the fretted note and A.H. are heard simultaneously.

**By Kenn Chipkin and Aaron Stang

RHYTHM SLASHES

STRUM INDICATIONS: Strum with indicated rhythm.

The chord voicings are found on the first page of the transcription underneath the song title.

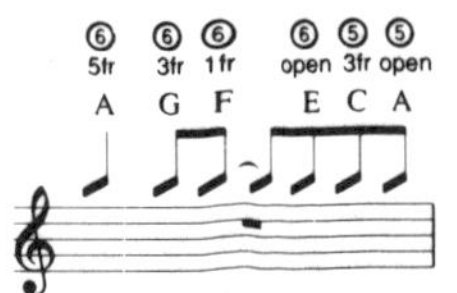

INDICATING SINGLE NOTES USING RHYTHM SLASHES: Very often single notes are incorporated into a rhythm part. The note name is indicated above the rhythm slash with a fret number and a string indication.

ARTICULATIONS

HAMMER ON: Play lower note, then "hammer on" to higher note with another finger. Only the first note is attacked.

LEFT HAND HAMMER: Hammer on the first note played on each string with the left hand.

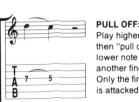

PULL OFF: Play higher note, then "pull off" to lower note with another finger. Only the first note is attacked.

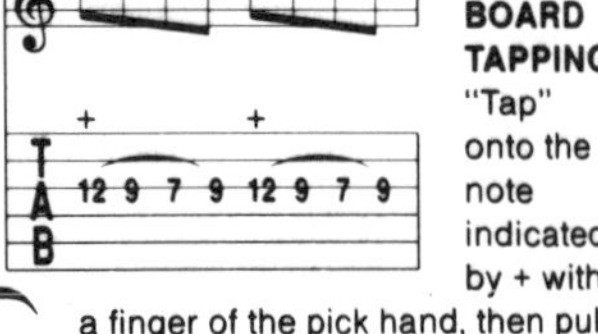

FRETBOARD TAPPING: "Tap" onto the note indicated by + with a finger of the pick hand, then pull off to the following note held by the fret hand.

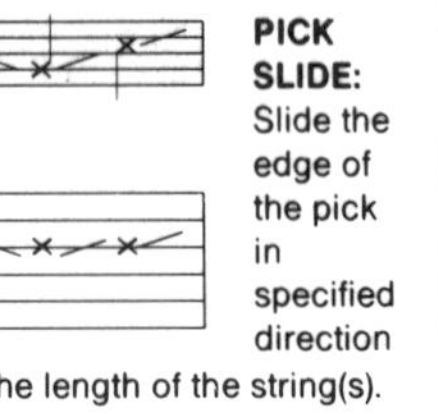

TAP SLIDE: Same as fretboard tapping, but the tapped note is slid randomly up the fretboard, then pulled off to the following note.

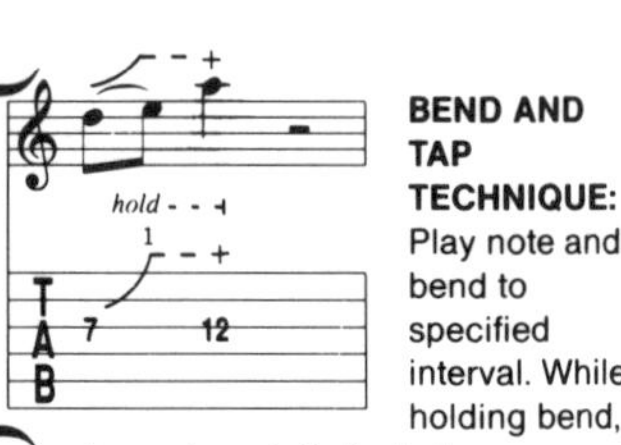

BEND AND TAP TECHNIQUE: Play note and bend to specified interval. While holding bend, tap onto note indicated.

LEGATO SLIDE: Play note and slide to the following note. (Only first note is attacked).

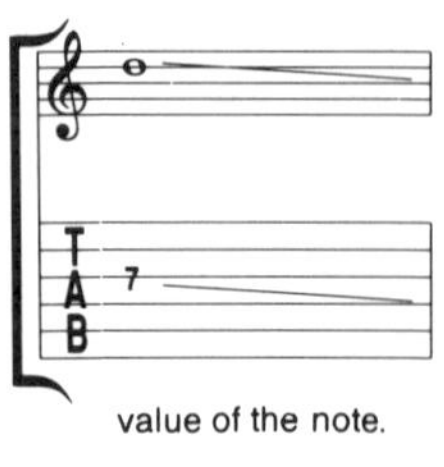

LONG GLISSANDO: Play note and slide in specified direction for the full value of the note.

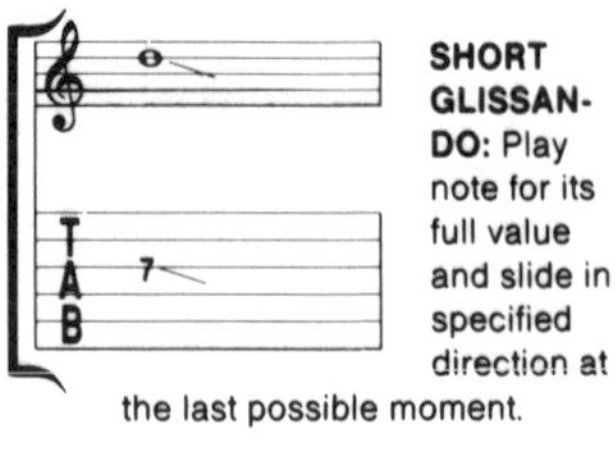

SHORT GLISSANDO: Play note for its full value and slide in specified direction at the last possible moment.

PICK SLIDE: Slide the edge of the pick in specified direction across the length of the string(s).

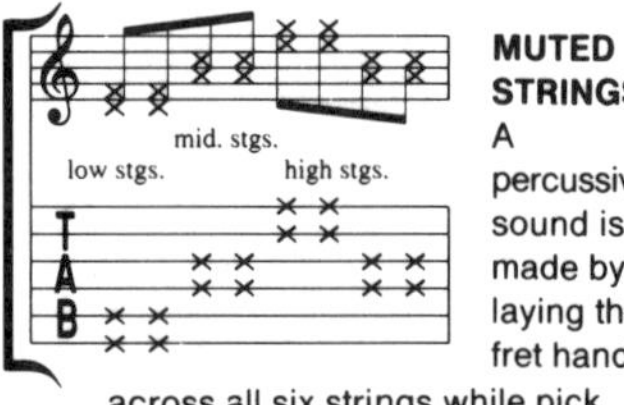

MUTED STRINGS: A percussive sound is made by laying the fret hand across all six strings while pick hand strikes specified area (low, mid, high strings).

PALM MUTE: The note or notes are muted by the palm of the pick hand by lightly touching the string(s) near the bridge.

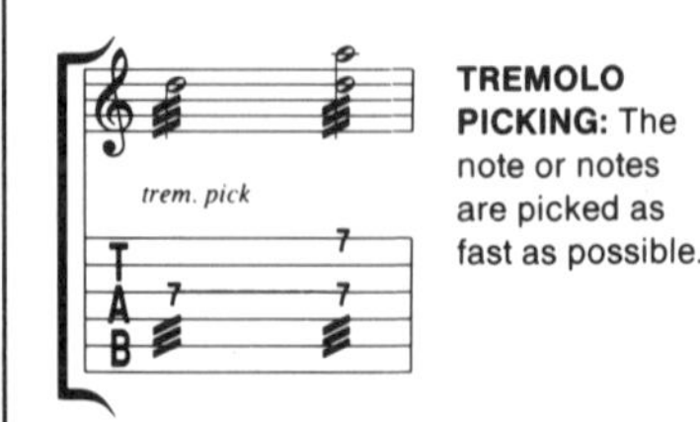

TREMOLO PICKING: The note or notes are picked as fast as possible.

TRILL: Hammer on and pull off consecutively and as fast as possible between the original note and the grace note.

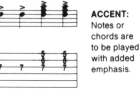

ACCENT: Notes or chords are to be played with added emphasis.

STACCATO (Detached Notes): Notes or chords are to be played roughly half their actual value and with separation.

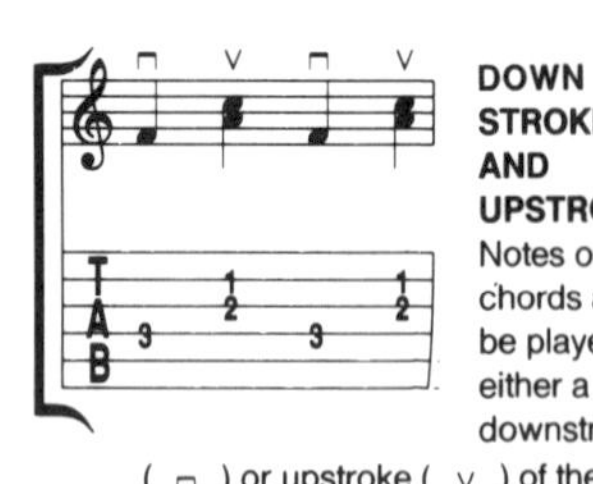

DOWN STROKES AND UPSTROKES: Notes or chords are to be played with either a downstroke (⊓) or upstroke (V) of the pick.

VIBRATO: The pitch of a note is varied by a rapid shaking of the fret hand finger, wrist, and forearm.